WHAT THEY ASK ABOUT MARRIAGE

WHAT THEY ASK ABOUT MARRIAGE

Raymond T. Bosler

AVE MARIA PRESS / NOTRE DAME / INDIANA 46556

Acknowledgment:

Universal Press Syndicate for permission to reprint in book form this selection of Msgr. Bosler's question-and-answer columns on marriage and related subjects.

Library of Congress Catalog Card Number: 75-11019
International Standard Book Number: 0-87793-096-1

Printed in the United States of America

Contents

part 1
Pre-Marriage

Pre-Marriage

WHY MARRIAGE?

Q. *My son has moved into an apartment with his girl friend. They are both mature and otherwise good people but they don't believe in marriage. They are deeply in love and say they want to stay that way forever, but they say love must be free and not smothered by constraint. When I prod him, my son admits that someday they may go through a marriage ceremony to protect themselves legally, but that first they want to grow in knowledge of each other, develop their love, which they feel they could not do unless they knew they were free to leave each other anytime they wanted. This very freedom, they think, will give them a better chance to succeed than the couples who go through all the formalities. How do I cope with this thinking?*

A. There is a basic human need which all the rapid changes of our technological age have not lessened in the least. Your son will probably recognize it best in the words of the Beatles: "Will you still need me, will you still feed me, when I'm sixty-four?" This, if I am not mistaken, is not a longing for security but a desperate cry for a love that is a commitment, a love that is faithful forever. So many modern songs express the fear that love will not last; they honestly reflect what is wrong in modern society: the lack of commitment and fidelity which are essential to true love.

Let's be honest. The institution of marriage has broken down with the prevalence of divorce. There is a lot of hypocrisy perpetrated at big church weddings, where brides and grooms promise to be faithful in sickness and in health until death, when everybody knows that if the union isn't happy an easy divorce by mutual consent will end it all. Our presidents lie to us; government leaders perjure themselves to hide their dishonesty; gigantic corporations help set up dictatorships in South America to protect their interests; the Church promises renewal and then seems to take two steps backward for each one forward. The young question the government, the Church and all institutions — today perhaps as never before because of the great explosion of knowledge in which they have grown up. They are idealists who dream of a Utopia in which all institutions disappear and man is free as the birds of the air. Unfortunately, life is not like our dreams. Governments and the Church will always be with us because humans require organization. All civilizations, however primitive, have required some public recognition of the union between man and woman and some form of ritual, to protect the rights of both parties and their children and because man seemingly must have it that way.

Your son probably is not aware that what he advocates is nothing new. Back in the 20's and 30's it was called "free love." One of the great proponents of that philosophy was Bertrand Russell. Yet this man recognized the need I have described when he wrote in his book, *Marriage and Morals:* "Most wholesomely constituted people desire, and will continue to desire, to have children; they will go on feeling that the best guardians of children are their parents living together in a permanent union. And when we put aside the question of children . . . and consider only the facts of personality, a permanent union is still required for development. In a series of transitory unions no two people can really ever know each other and all the possibilities each holds; they only take the first step on a road which beyond all others leads to the heart of life."

More directly touching the reasoning of your son on a trial marriage is this statement of Janet Golden, author of the *Quite Possible She* (Abbey Press, St. Meinrad, Ind.): "Learning to live together can be difficult enough, without adding the notion that one is somehow taken home on approval like a slightly doubtful dress from a department store. Admittedly, this may not be the way that the people concerned really see it. What they mistrust may not be the other person but the institution of marriage as they know it, and their commitment to each other may be unshakeable. But if it is not, then it seems to me that the absence of a genuine fidelity makes a very poor seed ground for the sort of personal growth that the two people are looking for."

Young people today talk much of personal fulfillment and they believe they will find it in sex, which they think of not as something dirty or sneaky but holy and fulfilling so long as it expresses love. But if historians and novelists and playwrights and psychologists have taught us anything at all about sex it is that it offers fulfillment only when it embodies perpetual fidelity. This is the lesson our young are going to have to learn the hard way.

PREMARITAL SEX

Q. *We are parents in our mid-40's and our five children range from late teens to mid-20's. We have been called "old fashioned," narrow-minded," "Victorian," etc., about our views on the "mod" idea of religion. We are very pleased with the changes in the Church, and our children would never miss Mass and are frequent communicants, but some of them haven't been to confession in two years. This worries us, as we thought everyone had to make his Easter duty. They say these laws are "passe," and one doesn't have to go to confession if he doesn't want to. Are the modern morals so much better than in the past? Is there no such thing as "iniquity" in the world anymore?*

A. Let's be honest about it. Not only the young, but the middle-aged, including priests and religious, are not going to confession as often as used to be the case. The Church as a whole, it seems, is searching for a better use of the sacrament of Penance. Some form of communal penance may ultimately be the answer. If one is offered in your locality, encourage your children to take part in it.

But, remember they are not obliged to go to confession unless they are aware of having committed serious sin. If they are receiving Communion frequently, then they are making their Easter duty. Confession is not part of the Easter duty except indirectly in the case of one in a state of serious sin.

I suspect that what bothers you — since you speak of the new morality — is that you fear your children are going along with the new sexual freedom and, therefore, in your own mind, making sacrilegious Communions. You may be unfair here, for though there is much more openness in speech and print about sex today and much freer association between the sexes, many of our young people live up to a sexual moral code as strict as their parents'. They may shock you by condoning what others are doing, but they may be more straightlaced than you in their personal lives.

Then, again, maybe they are sleeping where they shouldn't be and going on to Communion because they don't believe that what they are doing is sinful. (I have had several other parents ask about this problem.) You must do all you can to convince them they are wrong, but you ought not conclude they are guilty of sacrilegious Communions. You should give them the benefit of the doubt and decide they must be in good faith.

After all, there are respectable elderly adults who are weekly communicants even though they practice the worst kind of prejudice against people of other races. We presume they don't recognize the sinfulness of their actions. If we can give the benefit of the doubt to the exploiters of the poor and the corrupt politicians who have come forward for Communion in the past, surely we can extend the same courtesy to the young today, who may be confused about the morality of premarital sex.

This much we must say for the young. They may worry less about the sins of the flesh, but they are more worried about the victims of poverty and prejudice and more aware of the immorality of war and of their obligations to create a better world than we who were brought up on the old morality. The young are going through a difficult period of history when they are questioning the morality we have passed on to them. There is much in it to question. All we can do is hope that when they have finally recognized our failures and found something better to replace them, they will also have discovered we were right in some important matters.

Q. *Your answer to the parents alarmed because their teenagers were going to Communion without confession has caused much confusion. You wrote, "Maybe they are sleeping where they shouldn't be, and going to Communion because they don't believe what they are doing is sinful." Please explain the quote. I am assuming that these persons have heard of the Ten Commandments, or at least have had the Sixth Commandment explained to them, since you said that their parents had told them that their actions were sinful. Is it, then, permissible to form your own conscience concerning any of the commandments? This is what you seem to imply. I notice that you compare the sins of such persons to the sins of others in order to say in effect, "Don't worry, at least they're not that bad." Do you subscribe to the philosophy that all concepts are relative?*

A. No, I do not. I must not have made myself clear. I was not excusing the actions of the young people on the grounds that these were not as evil as other sins. I did not tell the young people to take lightly what they were doing. I advised the parents to give the benefit of the doubt to the youngsters. By this I meant they should assume the young people were in good faith when they held they were not sinning seriously by sleeping together.

As an example of what I meant, I pointed out that we do not always conclude that dishonest politicians or the prejudiced perpetrators of discrimination are guilty of sacrilege when they partake of Communion. We live in a culture where racial prejudice is common and a certain amount of dishonesty is taken as part of life. We can readily understand how a dishonest politician or a prejudiced employer could fail to recognize the evil of what he is doing, could fail to see he was breaking the commandments. Many of these persons are noble human beings in every other respect, good parents, generous and kind.

The boy and the girl who were the problem in the previous discussion were described by his father as good kids in every other way; they were good students in college, generous and sincerely interested in helping others. Could they in good faith have concluded that premarital sex was not sinful? Well, look at the world they are growing up in. Who writes the popular novels, who propagates the Playboy philosophy, who produces the films that are creating the new sexual morality? Not the teenagers. So the young aren't forming their own consciences. They are growing up in a society where there is a sexual revolution going on and the supporters of traditional morality are still arguing whether sex education should be given in the schools. It's easy to see how the young could confuse wrong for right. That's why I say we can give some of them, at least, the benefit of the doubt.

Having done that, we had better prepare ourselves to help them. Why is a marriage ceremony still necessary? What's wrong with premarital sex in the age of the pill? These are the kinds of questions which we have to prepare ourselves to answer intelligently.

Q. *In our sex-satiated society there is growing among teenage girls the concept that, since they reach the age of puberty at 13 or 14, it is natural and all right to have sexual intercourse prior to marriage. This concept exists even among girls who have had 12 years of Catholic education besides proper counseling by parents.*

What can a parent do to overcome this erroneous belief by a daughter when she can't be convinced that it is wrong and who goes to Communion regularly, apparently with no compunction about the sinfulness of fornication?

A. First, I would question just how "proper" the parental counseling was if it has no effect on a daughter's behavior. Certainly if she has any moral perspective she knows that sex outside marriage is wrong. Perhaps what your daughter is convinced of is that premarital relations are no longer fraught with the dangers they once were. Perhaps she thinks she is knowledgeable enough to avoid pregnancy or that, even if she should become pregnant, she will not be socially ostracized. She may believe that whatever happens her parents will "bail her out" and take the consequences for her.

But I would question whether teenagers today are any more immoral or amoral than those of any previous generation. Survey after survey among college students shows that young people still hold to traditional beliefs regarding sex and marriage.

The opportunities for violating those beliefs, however, are much more numerous. Certainly the entertainment media — movies, books and the like — are more suggestive and provocative. Too much assails decency, to say nothing of good taste. But "society" is not to blame entirely. Parents themselves are often responsible for their children's moral laxity. They emphasize "being popular," and a misguided girl may be deceived into believing popularity has to be bought with favors. Too many parents promote early dating and "going steady." They provide youngsters with their own cars or give them unlimited access to the family car. They may impose no limitations on hours or companions.

You do not state your daughter's age, but if you are unable to exercise your authority and convictions in this matter, seek the guidance of someone — perhaps your pastor or a school counselor — who can give you professional advice.

TEENAGERS AND SEXUALITY

Q. *I have asked my parents, consulted the bible and searched my conscience about this problem. I am confused to the hilt about the Sixth Commandment. What is an impure thought? Why is it wrong to think about sex when it is beautiful?*

A. Part of the problem with impure thoughts is that they are often confused with sexual thoughts. There is a difference. Since sex is a normal and necessary part of our human makeup, everyone has a sexual appetite just as he has an appetite for food, drink and rest.

These appetites will make themselves felt in us

whether we like it or not. Since we need food to live, we are going to think about food from time to time, even when we do not bring these thoughts on ourselves.

So, too, there are bound to be sexual thoughts crossing our minds from time to time. They may be spontaneous or they may arise from something we see or hear. There is nothing wrong with this.

A sexual thought becomes an impure thought when one deliberately dwells on it to such an extent that it gets out of hand. By that I mean that if a person consciously "holds" a thought in his mind with the intention of experiencing sexual gratification that he has no right to, then he is guilty of an impure thought. (The rights of husbands and wives, of course, are different from those who are not married.)

So the dividing line between normal sexual thoughts and impure thoughts depends upon one's intention and the way he handles these thoughts. If he deliberately brings them into his mind and deliberately keeps them there for the sake of sexual pleasure to which he has no right, then he has done wrong.

Sex is, indeed, a beautiful and noble part of God's creation and an important element of God's plan for man. But, like all good things, it can be misused. If one finds that sex, whether in thought or action, is for him simply a means of selfish gratification and tends to turn him in on himself rather than out to God and his neighbor in selfless love, if he separates sex from the order and beauty of God's design for man and reduces it to a mere animal instinct, then he is misusing one of God's gifts to him and frustrating his nature and purpose as a human being.

Q. *Is French-kissing a sin? I have asked this question before but got no answer. Don't we teenagers count? Please answer my question. The assistant pastor and the monsignor of my parish as well as other priests have said it is not a sin unless there is sexual involvement. But a missionary priest told us it was. And I don't see how it can be unless you are sexually aroused or it leads to a sexual act. If it is because it could lead to this then a regular kiss or just holding hands should be a sin too because it could lead to this. Please answer this as fast as you can. I must know the answer.*

A. The majority seems to be in your favor. Why are you so anxious to have another answer from me? Is it that deep down inside you, you suspect the lonely missionary priest is right? Monsignors have been known to be wrong before — as I can testify from bitter experience. I am inclined to think that yours was this time. Or you asked him the wrong question. Some years ago when I taught religion to high school girls I was plagued by this question. I put it to 12 young married couples and they unanimously agreed that French-kissing should not be indulged in by unmarried couples. Their reasons boiled down to this: young people would already be pretty much aroused before they would be ready to explore one another's mouths with their tongues.

However, it is a mistake to generalize in matters of sex. What is an occasion of sin for one may be quite innocent for another. You may be able to indulge in French-kissing without being unduly aroused. But what about the boyfriend?

The wrong about such liberties as you inquire about

is that for young unmarried couples they are not usually expressions of love but rather the exploiting of one another's body for pleasure. This is a poor preparation for married love.

Q. *I am 15 years old, and I think I have a serious problem. There is a priest I love very, very much, and every time I see him, which is about four times a year, I want to see him again and again. I would like to know if it is wrong to love a priest the way I do.*

A. Love is always an exciting experience. It is a good thing for you to love this priest, but it is important that you understand how and why.

It is a good thing to share many kinds of love in our life. We are made for loving. Our ultimate destiny is to love God forever. Therefore, we best use our lives by learning how to love. By experiencing many kinds of love we develop our capacity to love.

You have already experienced several kinds of love. Remember the love you may have had as a child, or maybe still have, for a puppy dog? Important as this may be, it doesn't compare with the kind of love you have for Mom and Dad, brother and sister. And I'll bet that as an 11- or 12-year-old girl there was, and maybe still is, a very special girl friend, a "soul sister" with whom you shared almost everything.

All these kinds of love are real and yet are different from one another. The love which you feel for this priest whom you see about four times a year is another love, real as can be, yet not to be confused with the love someday you will have for your husband.

Just at this point in your life you are looking for the

ideal man to love. Mother and father suddenly seem to
have so many faults and lack understanding. You tend
to idolize some person outside the family. It can be a
priest or a teacher or some other girl's father. It is better
that this happens than that you idolize some boy your
own age. This is how some girls get themselves rushed
into marriages before they know what love should be.

They see some young boy through the rosy glasses
of idolization and end up marrying a dream that bursts
when they discover what the boy is really like and that
neither he nor she was ready for marriage.

Your love for the priest, therefore, is good and can
be helpful if you do not confuse it with the love you hope
to have someday for your husband. This husband-wife
kind of love is unique. You want to be ready for it when
it comes. And you do this by being right now as fully
and loving a human person as you can possibly be. All
the loves of your life, from your first right down to this
latest love, are good preparations for the love of marriage — as it can, in turn, be for the love of heaven.

Q. *If you were married and had a 13-year-old girl and
she asked you: "What is love?" what would you answer?*

A. I think I would use the opportunity to help her discover in the scriptures how God himself has answered
this question. I'd read with her first from 1 John 4:7-21,
where we are told that God is love and that he has made
known what his love is by sending his Son to be one with
us. Consequently, I would urge her to become acquainted
with Jesus in the gospels, for in knowing him she knows
God and what love is. And then I'd show her how she

could check her own experience with love to see whether or not it is authentic or mere sentiment by reading St. Paul's great description of love in 1 Cor 13, especially: "Love is patient, love is kind. Love is not jealous, it does not put on airs, it is not snobbish. Love is never rude, it is not self-seeking, it is not prone to anger; neither does it brood over injuries. Love does not rejoice in what is wrong but rejoices with the truth. There is no limit to love's forbearance, to its trust, its hope, its power to endure."

Q. *I feel that when I get married I'd like to adopt all my children (if, of course, my husband feels the same way, otherwise I'll have some and adopt some). My father disagrees; he claims that marriage means bearing children. I say it's more important to bring up children, since just about any woman can bear children. I became aware of orphans and unhappy children and I'd like to show them a kind of home they'd never otherwise know.*

Will I be living in sin if I decide not to bear children even though I will have adopted several of them?

A. You had better pay attention to your father and think this problem through more deeply. Not every woman can have children. With the rapid drop in the birth rate and the alarming increase in abortions, there are very few infants up for adoption these days. Thousands of childless couples are desperately seeking infants to adopt. Have you thought of them?

Then consider that you are limiting your possibilities of marriage. The normal man wants children of his own. If you find a man who does not, the chances are he will not be generous enough to adopt any. If you enter a marriage with the intention of denying your husband the right to have children or limiting the right to one or two, the marriage would be invalid according to the teachings of the Church.

Finally, how can you reconcile your thinking with the Church's teaching that artificial means of birth control are wrong? It is true that there are many couples today who decide in good faith that the use of these means is justified as the only way they see it possible to avoid greater evils such as the breakdown of the mother's health or the breakup of a marriage. But it is hard to see how you could justify such actions on your grounds.

If you want to be generous, have children of your own and adopt an orphan from Vietnam or a black infant in need of a home.

PREGNANT GIRLS

Q. *I had to get married when I was 15 years old. We were married in church by a priest and my parents signed. They signed because that was the only out they could see. But at 15 did I really know what I was doing and, when you stop to think of it, did they have the moral right to sign my whole life away?*

There was a set of twin girls born out of that marriage. It lasted three years—three years of drinking and parties and beating up. I realize now that it takes two to make a mistake, but he was 20 to my 15.

We got divorced. I got it through the Church, and for a while I was content to just remain single for the rest of my life, but then I met this wonderful fellow who wanted to accept the twins as his own. We got married by a justice of the peace.

Well, we had our first baby, and right after that one of the twins died from open-heart surgery. She was only five years old, so I know I have a little angel in heaven rooting for us all the way. Then we had two more children, and my husband adopted the remaining twin. I am just 25 years old, and I went through three caesareans, a hysterectomy and a funeral in a little over three years. I'm not feeling sorry for myself, but how much does one have to pay back in this world?

When I first got remarried, religion didn't bother me too much, but now, as I'm getting a little older, I could just cry when I see families going to Communion together. You see, I do love my religion very much. All of our children are baptized Catholic and the twin has made her First Communion.

Why I write to you is to see if there is any hope. I know that you can't run around sinning and getting divorced and married two or three times, but can anybody be held responsible for something that happened at 15 years of age? It's bothering my parents quite a bit too, because they feel it's their fault for signing.

A. I print this letter, first of all, because it may prevent other young girls and their parents from making the same mistake. Marriage is not the only out for a girl in the predicament you were in. There are social agencies prepared to help a pregnant unwed girl find a place away from home to wait for her baby and then arrange for its adoption in a good home.

A girl's instinctive reaction is to want to keep her baby. But your experiences, and those of most other girls in similar circumstances, seem to prove that intellect, not instinct, should be in charge here as in every other important decision of life. Unfortunately, parents frequently lose their heads and work against the priest or minister advising against marriage in a case like yours.

But this is not helping you. Is there any hope that your marriage at 15 years of age could be declared invalid by the Church? There is a very good possibility that your youth and too much persuasion from your parents may have been obstacles to a valid matrimonial consent. I suggest you present your case to the matrimonial court of your own diocese. A priest of your parish can advise you on how to go about this.

Ecclesiastical judges are beginning to see defective consent in marriages like yours where they did not see it before. You have a good case.

Q. *I read your advice to girls in trouble suggesting they consider giving their child for adoption rather than rushing into a marriage that might not last. I must say you are all wet. A child isn't an old shoe or junk that can be thrown away.*

They tell you that some family will give them a better life. Well, maybe they don't care for a better life. Maybe they would rather know who they really are, who their folks are or what they are like and if they have any brothers or sisters.

On the other hand, maybe these young mothers who give up their babies when they get to be about 40 wonder too where their child is, whether she or he is alive or not, what they look like, etc.

A. What you say undoubtedly would be true in some instances. The many adoptive agencies around the country, however, could offer abundant evidence to prove

that your generalities are unfounded. The most essential
element for the success of any child is that it be brought
up in a home in which it is wanted and loved. Sometimes
the natural parent is not able to furnish such a home.
That's why there are so many adoptive agencies.

Q. *Our daughter advised us that she is pregnant and
the man responsible for this refuses to marry her.
What is the right thing to do for the baby's sake, the
mother's and all whose lives will be touched by this?
Should she give the baby up for adoption or keep it
and let it live the life of an illegitimate child?*

A. Though every case of this kind is unique, the odds
certainly favor the solution by adoption. The first consideration for a mother in such a situation is the happiness of the baby she is about to bring into the world.
Social agencies will find a good home where the baby
can, more than likely, have a better chance to grow up
normally than in the home of the mother's parents.

A child of this kind hampers the mother in her
chances of finding a husband and may find it difficult to
grow up under an eventual stepfather. Every sizable
city has homes for unwed mothers and social agencies
willing to take care of adoption procedures. I recommend this solution unless you have extraordinary reasons
for chancing the other. Too often in these situations the
mother and her parents don't want to give up "their"
baby; they place their own desires and emotions before
the future good of the child and frequently live to regret
their decision.

I am aware that this answer will bring me a letter or
two from mothers who were lucky enough to find

understanding men who became good fathers to their children, but the experience of most social agencies and pastors would, I think, argue in favor of adoption.

Q. *Where in the bible does it say that illegitimate children cannot enter the gates of heaven? Where in Church law does it state that "no female child adopted can become a nun"?*

A. Nowhere in the bible does it say that illegitimate children cannot enter heaven. There is no Church law forbidding religious orders to accept adopted children, male or female, legitimate or illegitimate. If there still are any religious orders or congregations that discriminate against adopted persons, the word ought to be spread around so that the young can put them out of business by looking elsewhere for a Christian order to join.

Q. *In a case where a girl has had a child out of wedlock, is she allowed to marry in the Church if she meets another Catholic who wants to marry her?*

A. Of course.

Q. *For many years I have wondered about the propriety of big weddings for pregnant brides. I concluded that God in his charity saw beyond the white gown, veil and celebrations and into the hearts of those being married and their families. It was none of my business, I thought, and God would be the judge. Then it became my business.*

Our daughter also had fallen like so many others.

In my grief and suffering, I asked, "Lord, what will you have me do?" The answer: "Love and forgive." But just what did that mean in this situation? Forgive as the father of the prodigal son had done, with joy and feasting? White symbolized purity, but joy, too. They who had sinned had asked for forgiveness and to be married before God in his Church. My thoughts went out to Mary Magdalene, a public sinner, washing the feet of Our Lord with her tears. She was among the first to share in the glory of the resurrection. And to Peter, weeping because he thrice denied the Master. Jesus gave him the keys of his kingdom and made him the head of his Church.

Reassured that truly "God is love," I placed all in the hands of the Father and prayed. I asked him to help the young couple become again like little children, letting God guide them through the rest of their lives, thus making their marriage grow into a true spiritual union.

With confidence we began preparations. There were moments of doubt, but we went ahead. We shall never cease being grateful to our pastor who made every effort to bring out the true meaning of Christian marriage. Our daughter was deeply touched. Through the years that memory will sustain her.

Without a large wedding we would not have experienced the great kindness of all those around us. Our family learned much about love and mercy, about suffering and grief shared together and offered to God in reparation. We did achieve real joy in celebration.

A.   Your outlook and the happy resolution of a difficult

situation should help others who may face a similar problem.

Q. *I have two young Catholic friends who had to be married. They made the mistake of not talking it over with their parents or their pastor and were married by a justice of the peace. Now what they want to know is, can they make their Easter duty?*

A. They cannot make their Easter duty unless they are properly married. Sometimes young people in this fix aren't sure they want to enter a permanent marriage. They marry before a justice of the peace to give the baby a name. Parents and relatives should not push them into rectifying their marriage with a church wedding. This is a problem they must work out for themselves with the help of a priest.

Q. *I would like to know what is the deal. I went to the priest and asked him to marry us next October. He said no because the girl is a high school senior this year. I was a senior last year. Father told us it wasn't permissible in our Church even for a couple who had to marry. But since he said this, he has married two senior girls, but they had to, and also the people had money, and we don't. It looks like we have to buy our way into the Church nowadays.*

A. I doubt that money had a thing to do with it. The parents of the girls in trouble may have pestered the priest into assisting at the marriages you referred to against his better judgment, because most priests, as far as I know, think that high school girls who get pregnant have a better chance for the happiness of the child and themselves if they give up the baby for adoption and wait until they are free to marry without pressure.

There can be exceptions. Some young couples give evidence that in spite of their mistake they have good chances of succeeding in an early marriage. Each case is different.

You can't know, and the priest can't tell you, why he decided to marry the two couples. You can be sure of one thing, he had your best interest at heart when he told you he didn't want to make arrangements to marry you while your fiancee is so young. He may think that both you and she need to enjoy your youth and freedom a little longer before taking on the responsibility and restrictions of marriage. And he and most sensible parents and all school officials know that seniors who are planning for marriage shortly after graduation do not benefit from their last year of high school as they should.

Then, again, the priest may be testing your seriousness; putting you off to see whether or not your desire to marry is the real thing or merely a teenage fantasy. If your parents think that you are ready for an early marriage, ask them to speak with the priest.

part 2

Marriage

Marriage

CATHOLIC MARRIAGES

Q. *Recently two supposedly good Catholics were married in a Catholic church and received Communion. Now the man says that he is an agnostic, that the girl agreed with him, that they had not been attending church. They defend themselves by saying that their wedding was in all honesty since it was a sanctioning of their love for each other in front of those who loved them and it would have been stupid to do otherwise just because they don't follow the Church's official line. Wouldn't that have been a sinful, dishonest and sacrilegious act?*

A. It could have been sacrilegious and no doubt, would have been had you or I done it. But in the case you described, the young couple may have done what they thought was the most charitable and sensible thing to do.

We must face the facts honestly. More and more young people today are refusing to commit themselves to the faith of their parents. They are not sure what they believe. They don't want to formally disassociate them-

32

selves from the church of their parents. They sense that marriage is something serious and sacred; therefore they want theirs to be solemnized in the church. They want their parents and friends present, who might not come or might be deeply hurt if the marriage took place before a justice of the peace. They mean no disrespect to their parents' and relatives' belief in the Eucharist. They may even be hoping that their own faith will revive at their wedding Mass. What does the priest do who suspects the couple preparing for marriage no longer fully believes in the Church and the sacraments? Should he refuse to let them marry in the church? This very likely would anger them and force them to a formal repudiation of the Church. There is always the hope that the young couple will have second thoughts as they mature and return to the faith of their youth. Any priest with experience knows that the sense of responsibility that the birth of children brings can make model parishioners out of young people who bragged of their agnosticism on their wedding day.

Personally I think we should sympathize with these young people and keep them as close to the Church as we can. And I cannot imagine that the Lord, who visited his enemies and sinners to eat with them, would in any way be offended by our allowing young people with doubts to approach him in the sacrament.

Q. *Can a marriage be called invalid if the words "I delegate you" were not said to the visiting priest by a priest of the home parish. This concerns a marriage which took place at a nuptial Mass, before the altar of God, in the presence of a priest, two witnesses and relatives and friends. All arrangements were made by the parish priest to have a dear friend of the family perform the ceremony. I maintain that any priest has the power to validly marry a couple and that the word "delegate" does not make the difference between a couple being married or not. I cannot see why a few words either give or take away the power of a priest to marry.*

A. The priest, strictly speaking does not marry a couple. The man and woman administer the sacrament of Matrimony to each other. The priest is but the official witness of the Church and of the State. To be an official witness he must observe all the requirements of Church and State.

To be the official witness of the Church a priest must be duly authorized. The fact that he is a priest does not automatically authorize him. In the usual parish the priests having the authority to witness marriages are the pastors and assistant or associate pastors. In the case of a visiting priest, the priests of the parish can, and, as you know, often do, delegate authority. This need not be any kind of formalized delegation or even put in writing. But the authority must be given if the marriage is to be valid. In the case you describe, the very fact that the pastor made the arrangements to have a priest friend of the family witness the marriage was delegation enough.

The purpose of the Church's marriage laws is to eliminate secret marriages. Hence, the public announcements of coming weddings (publication of the banns) and the requirement that those in charge of a church at least know about the wedding.

Q. *Suppose two Catholics had been previously mar-*

*ried in a Catholic church but one of the parties was
not in the state of grace at the time of the marriage.
Is this marriage recognized by the Church?*

A. Yes, it is. For the validity of a sacramental marriage it is not necessary that the contracting parties be
in the state of grace. The sinful party would receive a
valid sacrament but not the sacramental graces. The
graces would be available to him as soon as he repented
and sought forgiveness.

Q. *The man I want to marry was baptized and raised
a Catholic, but now he is an agnostic. I want to get
married in the Catholic Church, but I wonder if our
marriage in the Church would be valid if he does not
receive the sacraments of Penance and Holy Communion.*

A. You can marry this man validly in the Catholic
Church. He should not receive the sacraments of Penance and Holy Communion if he no longer believes. As
far as the sacrament of Matrimony is concerned, he is in
the position of any other baptized person who does not
believe matrimony is a sacrament. He would receive no
spiritual benefits from the sacrament but he would
validly contract marriage. Should he later revive his
faith, he could then begin to receive the spiritual benefits from the union, which was sacramental from the
beginning, even though he did not accept it as such at
the time of the marriage.

Q. *Is an alcoholic capable of contracting marriage?
I understand an alcoholic is often the victim of a phys-*

ical or mental disease. If he were drunk at the time of the marriage would it be a valid marriage?

A. If a person were so drunk at the time of the marriage ceremony that he did not fully realize what he was doing, he would be incapable of making a marriage vow. If he were so drunk that the next day he had no recollection of going through the ceremony, then surely the vow would be meaningless.

The fact that he is an alcoholic would not in itself make him incapable of pronouncing a vow. The question is: was he so drunk at the time of the ceremony that he did not know what he was doing?

Q. *Would you tell me if a marriage is valid in the sight of God when the couple is married at Mass without the grace of confession and Communion?*

A. So long as the two are free to marry and freely contract marriage, they would validly marry and receive the sacrament of Matrimony even though at the actual time of the marriage they are turned from God by sin unrepented. They would receive no spiritual benefits from the sacrament at the time of the marriage, but once they repented and wanted their marriage to be a sacramental source of divine help for their life in common, it would become that for them.

Marriage is a sacrament that perdures, and as man and wife are the ministers who give the sacrament to each other, so they continue throughout their life together to be the ministers of grace to each other.

Q. *Recently a friend told me of a Catholic wedding she attended in Chicago where the bride and groom*

*lit the candles and later a marriage candle was lit from
the original candles. Can you give any details on how
this would be done, the significance, or where a marriage candle can be obtained?*

A. This is a custom that has been common in some
Protestant churches. The lighting of the candle from
two other lights signifies the fusion of the two lives. This
ceremony is done at the very end of the service. It is an
effective symbol of the unity of marriage.

The candle is sometimes called an anniversary
candle because of the custom of preserving it in a prominent place in the home and lighting it each year on the
anniversary of the wedding. These candles can be
purchased in religious goods stores and in some bridal
sections of department stores.

Q. *At a recent "posh" wedding the bride's parents
employed a harpist to play "When Irish Eyes Are Smil-
ing" during the ceremony. While it was beautiful, different, the question arises: Since when is "Irish Eyes"
considered church music, or is it? To me it was out
of place. To others it was OK.*

A. "Irish Eyes" is not church music. It would be out of
place and probably forbidden by church music com-
missions to use the song during liturgical services. But
the harpist, I presume, was playing before the bride
came down the aisle, putting the people waiting in the
proper mood. A wedding is an occasion for joy and
gaiety. I personally think that the familiar melody of
"Irish Eyes" played with dignity by a harpist could set
the proper mood for an Irish wedding. It would, of

course, be monstrously improper for a Polish, Italian or German wedding.

PARTICIPATING IN OTHER WEDDINGS

Q. *Recently my nephew married in a Lutheran church. The parents, very hurt, went to see several priests. All told them not to have anything to do with the wedding, not to attend any part, which includes showers and wedding reception. It was hard for them, but they did it. Several aunts, uncles and cousins (all supposedly good Catholics) just couldn't stay away, knowing that the parents, grandparents and the others weren't going. They're saying: "What's the difference, what's done is done," and "How do we know that our faith is the one true faith?" We were always taught that it was wrong to attend, that by attending you were approving the wrong being done. Has the Church changed its standing on this or is it still a sin?*

*   *   *

Q. *There have been many conflicting opinions in our family on the following situation: What is the Catholic Church's stand on (1) the participation of Catholic relatives in the wedding, and (2) the attendance of Catholic relatives and friends at a wedding where the bride left her Catholic Church and the groom left his Protestant church and they both joined and are being married in another Protestant church?*

A. This is a problem that seemingly is on the increase. The two questions above came from Wisconsin and Texas. I have received similar questions from Louisiana,

Iowa, New York and Indiana. I chose the above because they both reflect a difference of opinion within families over what should be done today.

A generation ago staunch Catholic families would have been united in support of the advice of the priests to boycott any marriage ceremony where a Catholic relative was vowing himself out of the Church. If this is no longer the case, it is not necessarily because the faith of Catholic people is weakening; it may be that changing circumstances call for a whole new approach to this problem.

The reasons for attending the wedding given by the aunts and uncles of the Catholic boy married in the Lutheran church were certainly wrong, but that does not mean that the advice given by the priests would be good advice for every contemporary family.

In a small German community, where Lutherans and Catholics live side by side, a marriage like that described above would be the talk of the town and the attendance of close relatives might look like capitulation on the part of the Catholics.

These ethnic communities are remnants of what Catholic life used to be here in the United States. They can afford considerable support to the Catholic faith and morals of their young through the social pressure they exert upon them. But they are indeed the exception today.

The vast majority of our Catholics now live in cities where population turnover is frequent and family ties are loose. At weddings today, where relatives come from all over the country, few people know much about one another. The possibility of giving scandal by seeming to condone the sinful action of one's child or relative by attending his wedding outside the Church would be limited. To those who do know the circumstances it is possible to explain one's displeasure and disagreement with the decision of the young person.

More scandal might be given today by what might appear to be complete lack of love and interest in their children were the parents to cut themselves off from the wedding.

It seems to me that the determining factor here is how can the faith of the son or daughter or relative best be saved. Will my refusal to attend the wedding induce the young person to rectify his mistake and return to the practice of his faith or alienate him from the faith and the family forever? If I explain the Catholic position as best I can to the future in-laws and then go along with the wedding and celebrations with the best front I can muster, will I not in the long run have a better chance of keeping close to the young couple so that I can be an influence in their future?

I cannot answer these questions for you. No priest can. This is your decision. It is not always an easy one.

Q. *We are Catholic and are invited to a Protestant wedding. Is it wrong to go? They are the best of friends and neighbors.*

A. They won't be, if you don't act like a friend and neighbor. Go to the wedding.

Q. *Please print, verbatim, the Church law which forbids a Catholic from attending his grandson's or nephew's wedding (or a son for that matter) when that person marries a Methodist in the Methodist church before a minister.*

A. There is no such law. Catholic moral theologians have long taught that it is wrong to cooperate in the sin of others. They distinguished between direct and indirect cooperation—between, say, holding the gun while a companion robbed a bank or lending the robber your gun. Marrying outside the Church would usually be sinful. A parent who would encourage a child to do this would be directly and sinfully cooperating in the sin. A parent or relative who tries to discourage such a sin and makes his disapproval known would be only indirectly cooperating by attending the wedding. There are times when indirect cooperation is excusable. It might, for instance, be better to attend the wedding you describe, for by staying away you might cut yourself off from any influence over the relative marrying out of the Church.

It seems to me that the question you must ask yourself in every case of this kind is how can you best help the relative. Will your refusal to attend the wedding induce the young person to rectify his mistake and return to the practice of his faith, or alienate him from the faith, and the family forever? In the situation in which we live today, I think that most people will decide that nothing is gained by staying away. But each case is different and must be decided on its own merits.

Q. *Do you think I am wrong in believing that each person has the right, indeed, actually the duty, to prayerfully reflect on and decide what his own religious beliefs are, regardless of the profession and teachings of his parents?*

Therefore, when one's Catholic relatives marry in a Protestant church, would it not be the Christian attitude to assume they are acting in good faith? Do we

*really have the right to judge that those who "marry
outside the Church" are committing sin?*

A. You and I are pretty close to seeing eye to eye. We
agree that people must make the faith their own and
that we should presume that others act in good faith
until we have solid reasons for thinking the opposite.

There are cases, however, perhaps many of them,
when a Catholic reluctantly gives up allegiance to his
Church to marry someone unwilling to marry on any
other terms. This is a sinful choice which such persons
may regret the rest of their lives.

But, I agree with you that young Catholics today can
in good faith decide that the Catholic religion as they
experienced it at home or in some particular locality no
longer is meaningful for them or does not reflect for them
the gospel message as well as some Protestant church
they are attracted to. This is no admission that the
Protestant church is better than the Catholic, but rather
that the faith as lived in a particular Catholic home or
taught by particular religious teachers was inadequate.

I present this as only my own opinion, for there are
theologians who would fall back upon the traditional
Catholic teaching that the faith cannot be lost except
through one's own sinful fault and maintain that no one
can leave the Catholic Church without sinning. My
answer to this is that I do not think that all Catholics who
join a Protestant church necessarily lose the gift of faith.

The gift of faith is a grace from God that enables us
to believe and live by the Christian revelation. Sometimes, unfortunately, Catholics can learn such a distorted
notion of the Christian revelation in their homes or
schools that they reject it and find what their faith helps

them want in other churches—not the fullness of the Christian revelation they might have found in the Catholic religion had they learned it properly, we Catholics would say, but nevertheless enough to be the true object of their faith.

Indeed, we Catholics ought to be disappointed and sorrowful when one of our own leaves the Church, but not so much because we fear such a one has lost all faith but because we realize we have failed to present the Catholic Church in all its fullness and glory.

Q. *What is a parent to do with a beloved daughter who has left the Church and become a Baptist? She intends to marry a Baptist in his church. We sent her to a Catholic college for four years. We are heartbroken. She is heartbroken because we will not attend her wedding and her father cannot give her away.*

This family who once loved one another so have now split. Why? Because of religion. Our faith forbids us to go to the wedding. She is our daughter; we love her. Is this what God intended, to let different faiths tear a family apart?

God's great commandment is love. How is love going to survive when the Church tells a mother she cannot attend her daughter's wedding? We love our daughter. We love our Catholic faith. It hurt terribly when she left our faith. Which way do we turn?

A. You may find the solution to your problem in my previous answer. But supposing you are convinced your daughter is in bad faith and she has let her love for her fiance so overwhelm her that she has sinfully left her Church, do you think the Christian thing to do is sever all relations with her? I don't think so. The Church does not forbid you to attend her wedding; the Church forbids you to act as though you think it doesn't matter what she believes or what church she belongs to.

You have, obviously, made your mind clear to her. I think you can attend the wedding without compromising your own convictions. You can make clear to the in-laws how you feel without offending them. And if your daughter is acting against her conscience, you will be able to help her rectify it someday if you stay close to her. If you cut yourself off, you'll never be able to help her.

Follow your heart in this instance, is my advice. Other priests may disagree with me. Consult with others before making your decision.

Q. *What is the official position of the Catholic Church today regarding the marriage of a Catholic to a non-Catholic in a Protestant church without the presence of a priest? Should Catholics refuse to attend such a ceremony and refuse to acknowledge the so-called marriage with a gift? I have always felt that to go along with it is a silent condoning of such a wedding. We are finding today that the thinking on this varies from one parish to another. Some priests tell their parishioners it is all right to go to keep peace in families. Others say, "Well, you really shouldn't, but use your own judgment." What has become of the authority that we were always taught was the cornerstone of our faith?*

A. You bring up so many problems at once that I hardly know where to begin. The authority of the Church is still intact, though somewhat wobbly because those who exercise it and those who obey it have not yet learned how to make the change from a highly regulated, closed society of uneducated peasants or immigrants to an open, democratic society of self-reliant, educated citizens brought up to make decisions for themselves.

Authority over children is one thing; authority over adults is quite another. In the past, popes, bishops and pastors had to make detailed practical applications of moral principles to concrete cases for a people incapable of making them for themselves. In those days priests wanted to go to a canon law or a moral theology book to find a clear answer to every moral problem, and the people wanted from the priest a clear "yes" or "no" answer to the question: "Is it a sin, Father?" This worked well in a simple culture where all were of the same faith and community pressure helped support the moral decisions made by church authorities. But this no longer holds true today for us in our pluralistic society. Your problem is a good example of the difference.

When Catholics lived in a ghetto (territorial or psychological), it was probably best for priests to forbid taking part in a marriage of a child or relative "outside the Church," for this undoubtedly prevented many such marriages from taking place and helped keep intact the Catholic community so necessary then to preserve the faith of immigrants in an alien culture. The situation is not the same today, and the prohibition against attending marriages of Catholics outside the Church is no longer effective in applying social pressure to keep the young in line. Sometimes it could do more harm than good.

Every case is different. Parents and relatives will have to make their own decision. "How can the faith of the person best be saved?" That's the first question they must ask themselves. Will their refusal to have anything to do with the wedding shock the person into realizing the mistake or alienate him or her from the faith and the family forever?

"Is there danger of giving scandal by seeming to condone the sinful action by cooperating in a marriage outside the Church?" That's the second and balancing question. In these days of greater independence of children and loss of parental control, Catholic friends and relatives will ordinarily understand and sympathize with the parents in their dilemma and take no scandal at cooperation in the wedding. And it is quite possible that more scandal might be given to Protestants by what could appear to be a lack of love and interest in their child were the parents to avoid the wedding. For a better understanding of this, moreover we must keep in mind that our Church now does give permission for a Catholic to be married in a Protestant church without a priest present and that those attending a given wedding would not know whether it was performed with or without Church permission.

When in doubt as to what to do in these situations, it seems to be better to choose the course that will keep parents, friends and relatives close to the one who "marries outside the Church."

Q. *The son of a Catholic friend of ours was divorced and soon will be married again in a Protestant church with a large wedding. Part of our family may be asked to participate, but we are reluctant because of the anti-Catholic circumstances. Are we being old-fashioned? Personally I feel guilty in even thinking about going*

and am hoping and praying something occurs to ex-
cuse our presence.

A. By all means, find an excuse if you feel guilty about attending the wedding. But need you? What are the anti-Catholic circumstances? Since it is impossible for the marriage to take place in a Catholic church, the girl is certainly not anti-Catholic because she wants the wedding in her own church. You, of course, do not want to put your approval upon the action of the man who enters a second marriage contrary to the laws of his Church. Will your attendance at the wedding do this? You must decide this for yourself. If the family knows what your own convictions are concerning marriage, they will more than likely understand that your presence at the wedding is a gesture of friendship toward them and not a con-doning of the action of their son.

Q. *A friend of mine has fallen away from the Catholic faith and joined a Protestant faith and is now planning to be married to a member of this community. She has asked me to be an attendant at their marriage. Is it right for me to do so? I was told that as a Catholic I could attend the wedding of another religion but not be a part of the wedding. I do not know if I should accept what my friend has done about her religion, but as a friend and out of kindness do not wish to cause any hurt feelings.*

A. The Church now has no objections to your being an attendant at a Protestant wedding. However, you have a decision of your own to make. If your friend left the Catholic Church and joined another just to get her man, you should ask yourself whether you would help or harm her more by refusing to be an attendant. By refusing her will you make her aware of the fact she has done something wrong or repel her further from the Catholic Church? By being kind to her, and thereby remaining close to her, will you be in a better position to help her return to the Church? These are questions you must ask yourself before deciding what you should do. And don't forget to ask yourself how others may react to your taking part in the ceremony.

If your friend had gradually drifted away from the Catholic Church — probably because she never really was committed to it — and found in the Protestant Church what she thought she needed, then you may presume she was in good faith and you have no problem at all.

Q. *Are you allowed by the Catholic Church to attend a wedding at a Jehovah's Witness Hall between two Jehovah's Witnesses?*

A. Yes.

MIXED MARRIAGES

Q. *Could something be printed regarding mixed marriage laws? Since each diocese seems to have a different set of rules, and we read so much of Catholics being married in Protestant churches and Protestants being able to officiate at marriages, it is all very confusing.*

Also, are other churches making as many changes as we are, pertaining to mixed marriages?

A. The bishops at Vatican Council II, seemed to be in general agreement that the Church law on mixed marriages needed to be revised. The recommendations of the Council gradually have been put into effect so that at the present time the following regulations prevail:

1) Catholics who contract a mixed marriage before a Protestant minister are no longer excommunicated, although the marriage is still invalid.

2) However, bishops may grant a dispensation from the Catholic form of marriage so that a Catholic may validly marry before a Protestant minister, a Jewish rabbi, or even a justice of the peace, when there are good reasons for granting the dispensation. Such reasons could be: to achieve family harmony, or avoid family alienation, to obtain parental consent, to permit marriage in a church that has a particular importance for the non-Catholic. A dispensation from the impediment of mixed religion or disparity of cult must also be obtained for this, and the marriage is recorded in the parish of the Catholic party and in the office of the bishop granting the dispensation.

3) A non-Catholic minister may be present at a mixed marriage in a Catholic church and may read the scriptures, say prayers and give a blessing. However, only the priest receives the marriage vows.

4) A mixed marriage may be celebrated during a nuptial Mass with the blessings, but the desires of the non-Catholic family must be respected.

5) The responsibility for the baptism and Catholic upbringing of the children rests with the Catholic partner, who is asked to promise to do all in his power to raise the children in the Catholic faith. No promises are required of the non-Catholic party, who, nevertheless,

must be informed of the promise made by the Catholic.

The Protestant churches share our anguish over the problem of mixed marriages, and they recognize that these changes do not solve all the difficulties. Only Christian unity will do that. In Europe several Protestant churches have forbidden their pastors to take part in mixed marriages in a Catholic church, reasoning as the Synod of the Reformed Church in France put it: "such a practice, even though authorized from charitable intentions, can only favor confusion and misunderstandings by suggesting a 'double blessing.'" In our own country, some Lutheran Churches prohibit their pastors from being present at such marriages or allowing a Catholic priest to take part in a marriage in a Lutheran church.

My personal experience is that most Protestant ministers, including Lutheran pastors, have been most cooperative and pleased with the possibilities our new regulations offer.

Q. *My niece was married in a Catholic church to a Lutheran. Recently they had a child born to them which they had baptized in a Lutheran church. Does this excommunicate her from the Catholic Church?*

A. No, it does not excommunicate her, but it may very well mean she has of her own accord joined her husband's church. Or, it may mean that her husband prevailed, and she decided it was better to have the child baptized in his church rather than not baptized at all. In this case, she need not consider herself cut off from the sacraments; she should be faithful to her religious duties, be the best Christian mother she can, and be the peacemaker of her family. Children who become the center of a bitter religious dispute often grow up without any religion.

Q. *Twenty years ago I was married in the Church to a wonderful Protestant man, who will not turn Catholic for me. The reason is because he refuses to believe the Blessed Mother was a virgin when she conceived and bore Christ. He says when the Catholic Church stops her "fairy tales" he'll turn Catholic for me. Is it true the Dutch Catechism questions the virgin birth? I would so love to have my husband turn Catholic for me in our declining years.*

A. Let's hope that if he does turn Catholic it will not be for you but for God. You had better be grateful your husband is a good man, for from the looks of things you are going to live with him a long time before he decides to "turn."

I suspect the virgin birth is not the only Catholic "fairy tale" for your husband. To believe that Jesus of Nazareth is both God and man, that he rose from death to a life gloriously above all the laws of matter and still remains human, that he is present in the appearances of bread and wine in the Eucharist — these are all harder for man with his earthbound knowledge to accept than the virgin birth — something which man, all by himself, may soon be able to duplicate.

The belief in the virgin birth is based upon the gospel accounts of the birth of Jesus and the long traditional interpretation of these accounts common to all the churches. The Dutch Catechism and other recent writings by Catholics that do throw some doubt on the virgin birth do so not because it is a fairy tale and impossible to believe but because some theologians feel that Jesus would be more like us in his humanity if he had a human father. They think that the scriptural reference to a virgin birth was merely a Hebrew way of stressing the fact that God had a special hand in the birth of Jesus. The official Church does not agree with this.

Q. *A devout Methodist woman and a devout Catholic man were first married civilly. After the first child, a boy, was born, they remarried in the Catholic Church. This was agreed on after much deliberation, counseling by a Catholic priest and a Methodist minister and thoughtful prayer. This was in the mind of the woman a great sacrifice, but she loved her husband and wanted his peace of mind. This first and a subsequent boy were baptized as Catholics. They and the father regularly attend Mass, the mother still remaining a devout Methodist.*

She wants desperately to have a little girl and to bring her up in her own Methodist faith. She has a near neurotic obsession over this which brings much mental anguish when the subject is brought up, which is quite frequently. Can the husband out of love and concern for his wife allow his daughter to be baptized in the Methodist Church without endangering his own soul?

A. Your question would have been much more difficult to answer a few years ago than it is now. Then the Protestant spouse in a mixed marriage was required to promise to bring up all children in the Catholic faith. Today, however, the Catholic Church recognizes that there can be problems of conscience for the Protestant spouse. No longer does she require promises from the Protestant party, and from the Catholic party she requires only that he or she sees to it "as far as possible" that the children be baptized and brought up in the Catholic faith.

The changes in regulations regarding mixed marriages were made to take care of situations like the one you describe. The Catholic man has gone "as far as possible." If he goes any further, he may endanger the marriage; or at the very least, he may force his wife to go against her conscience. Some compromise is obviously necessary. He may find it easier to make this compromise if he reflects upon the teaching of Vatican Council II that those who though they are not Catholics "believe in Christ and have been properly baptized are brought into a certain, though imperfect, communion with the Catholic Church." (Pope Paul himself referred to this passage when promulgating the new regulations on mixed marriages in 1970.)

What I am suggesting here is not a guideline for all mixed marriages for most Protestant spouses find it to be in the best interests of the religion of the children to support the Catholic party in bringing up all the children as Catholics. This they can do without going against their consciences and seemingly without any unbearable sacrifice.

Q. *Two years ago my brother-in-law, a non-practicing Catholic, was married to a non-Catholic by a justice of the peace. After the recent birth of their first child they tried to make arrangements to have the baby bap-*

*tized as a Catholic. Their pastor refused to baptize
the baby unless the parents were remarried in the
Church. Is this normal Church policy? If so, I think it
is a mistake. The parents already consider themselves
married, as they feel marriage is basically a promise
two people make to each other. It seems to me that
the pastor should have been happy they showed an
interest in baptizing the baby. Instead he has antago-
nized them, driving them further from the Church.*

A. The pastor in this case was faced with a delicate
problem. Why does this nonpracticing Catholic want
his baby baptized in the Catholic Church? Merely to
conform to a social or family custom? Merely to make his
own Catholic mother happy? These would not be
sufficient reasons. For what the priest needs to know is
whether the parents intend to bring the child up in the
Christian faith.

In the baptismal ceremony the priest must ask them
whether they accept the responsibility of training the
child in the practice of the faith. Before he agrees to
baptize the child, therefore, he must know whether or
not the couple can sincerely accept such a responsibility.
And what he needs to know above all is the attitude of
the father in this case toward the Catholic Church.

If the man is serious about rearing the child in the
Catholic Church, then he ought to be willing to regulate
his marriage according to the rules of that Church. It is
not the whole truth to say that he and his wife "feel
marriage is basically a promise two people make to each
other," for they recognize that this promise had to be
acknowledged and regulated by the state; they got a
license and made their promises before a justice of the

peace. If he is a Catholic, then he should be willing to recognize the authority of his Church and her right to regulate marriage. If he no longer believes the Church has this right and authority, then in all honesty he should no longer profess to be a Catholic.

In a situation like this, I wouldn't bluntly confront the man with an ultimatum, "You cannot have your baby baptized until your marriage is rectified." This might pressure him into doing something he would rather not do. I would insist upon a lengthy conversation with the mother as well as the father. Here the peculiar circumstances of the case will surface and, with the proper instruction, the couple can be helped to see how the Church looks upon baptism and marriage and led to make their own decision.

There is no general policy of the Church forbidding the baptism of children whose parents are not willing to be married in the Church. It would be imprudent for a diocese or a parish to make such a policy, it seems to me, for each case of this kind is unique and must be decided as a pastoral problem by the good sense and prudence of the individual pastor.

CATHOLIC-PROTESTANT

Q. *A near relative of ours who is a Catholic married a Protestant girl before a justice of the peace. Is it a church law and is it mandatory to have such a marriage "blessed," to use the vernacular of the people? Is there a church penalty against the Catholic partner for not having the Catholic ceremony? Is the procedure to have the "blessing" performed by a priest very intricate?*

A. Your relative is married civilly to the Protestant girl, but according to the laws of the Catholic Church he is not properly married. Our Church requires a special form for marriages. To be united in what the Catholic Church considers a permanent, valid marriage, a Catholic must marry before an authorized priest and two witnesses. The purpose of this law is to prevent hasty and ill-prepared marriages.

The Church does not question the legal effects of the marriage of a Catholic before a justice of the peace and would not permit such a person to marry in the Church until a civil divorce had been obtained. Once the divorce is obtained, however, the Church would allow another marriage. Thus a young Catholic who against the advice of parents and pastor entered an ill-matched marriage before a justice of the peace and shortly thereafter sought relief from it in the divorce courts would not be in the position of one who could never marry again or if married would be cut off from the sacraments.

If your relative is serious about his marriage and wants to be altogether sincere with his wife, he will arrange with a priest to make his civil promises binding also in the Church. This is a very simple ceremony. The priest will have to give several instructions to the wife to acquaint her with the principal beliefs and duties of her Catholic husband and help her decide whether or not she can come to some agreement on the Catholic upbringing of the children. This is necessary before the priest can obtain a dispensation from his bishop for the marriage. But this is routine for any mixed marriage between a Catholic and a Protestant.

So long as your relative lives with his wife without

validating the marriage, as we say, in the Church, he may not receive the sacraments. This is the penalty imposed upon him for his manner of living.

Q. *Now that Catholics who marry before a Protestant minister are no longer excommunicated, may Catholics who have already married in this way enjoy all the privileges of the Church, such as receiving Holy Communion and Christian burial? Does the marriage have to be performed by the priest?*

A. Though the penalty of excommunication is lifted, Catholics are still bound to the Catholic form of marriage, that is: they must be married before a qualified priest and two witnesses before the marriage is valid. To enjoy the privileges of the Church, therefore, one who has married outside the Church must first have the marriage validated before a priest.

Q. *How can the Church consider marriage between a Catholic and another Christian which does not take place before a priest invalid? Is it not the two Christians themselves who administer the sacrament to each other? I thought the Church could never affect the validity of a Christian marriage, only the lawfulness of one, through Church laws.*

A. It is true that the two exchanging marriage vows administer the sacrament of Matrimony to each other. But precisely because Christian marriage is a sacrament, the Church believes she has the right and obligation to determine what is necessary for the valid conferring of this as of the other sacraments.

At present, Church legislation requires for the validity of a marriage in which one party is a Catholic that the vows must be exchanged before an authorized priest, as the official witness of the Church, and two other witnesses. The authorized priest is the pastor of the place where the marriage is performed or the bishop or vicar general of the diocese or a priest designated by these.

I said "at present" since prior to 1908 there was no general law throughout the whole Church requiring the celebration of marriage before an authorized priest for validity. And prior to the Council of Trent in the 16th century nowhere in the Roman Catholic Church were marriages contracted outside the Church considered invalid. They were forbidden and unlawful, but, nonetheless, valid.

The Church could very well return to the older discipline and no longer demand the present form as necessary for validity. In fact, for good reasons even now the Church will dispense from the requirement and accept as valid a marriage of a Catholic in a Protestant church. Permission for this must be sought from the bishop.

Q. *Would you please explain how a Catholic could be married in an Episcopalian church by the Episcopalian pastor and a Catholic priest. The bride was the Episcopalian. Both pastors were reported as performing the ceremony.*

A. The pastors were only the official witnesses of their two churches. The couple exchanging vows married themselves. The only performance the pastors were capable of was blessing the marriage and conducting the ceremony by reading the scriptures and directing the proceedings.

Our bishops may grant permission for a priest to witness the exchange of wedding vows of a Catholic and a person not a member of the Roman Catholic Church in the church of the latter. The Catholic form of marriage is still observed, for the priest is there as official witness of the Church. Or the bishop may dispense from the Catholic form of marriage, so that the non-Catholic minister could accept the vows and the Catholic priest be present to read the scripture passages usual assurances that children will be brought up as and give a blessing. And for the present, at least, the Catholics must be previously made and a dispensation granted.

I say "for the present at least" since we do not know what the future will bring. The Catholic attitude toward mixed marriages has been and still is an obstacle to better relations between Catholics and Protestants. Protestants generally feel that the demand the children be raised as Catholics is an infringement of the religious rights of the Protestant in a mixed marriage. There are Catholic leaders, bishops and theologians, especially in Europe, who would agree. They would eliminate the promises and let the couple themselves determine in time what religion the children embrace. They have two principal reasons: 1) the marriage partner with the stronger faith and religious convictions will more than likely influence in the end the religious development of the children, promises or no promises, and 2) because of insistence on the promises many couples today contract civil marriages and both give up any serious practice of religion.

Q. *Can a Catholic boy and a Protestant girl be married in a Protestant church with both priest and minister present? The girl plans to join the Catholic Church later. Her mother wants the wedding and reception at her church. A priest has told them they can as long as the Catholic fulfills his obligations as a Catholic. I never heard of this before.*

A. This is indeed something new. The local bishop can now give permission for such a wedding.

Q. *My brother recently was married to a lovely non-Catholic girl. At the last moment before the wedding the officiating priest informed him that the bride could take Communion at the nuptial Mass if she wished to do so. This surprised me, pleasantly. But the 11th-hour notification did not allow enough time to prepare for such a privilege. Is it the usual thing now for the non-Catholic party to take Communion at such a time?*

A. No. Some years ago Rome did grant this privilege for a marriage that took place in Italy. The Protestant bride, however, had expressed her intention to embrace the faith and was taking instructions at the time. The Vatican expressly stated that the permission was not to set a precedent.

I personally am most unhappy with the present arrangement of allowing a nuptial Mass for a mixed marriage and yet not permitting the Protestant spouse to receive Communion. It is awkward and inconsistent, to say the least, to offer Christ in the host to the Catholic spouse and pass by the Protestant, who just a few minutes before had performed as the minister of Christ in giving the sacrament of Matrimony to the Catholic. And that's what we Catholics believe: that the Protestant in such a marriage is the minister of the sacrament of Matrimony. The spouses are the ministers in matrimony, not the priest.

It seems to me that so long as the Protestant asks for it and believes somehow Christ is present in the sacrament (even though not understanding what Catholics mean by transubstantiation), he or she could be given Communion on this one exceptional occasion of the nuptial Mass without opening the way to what is known as Inter-Communion.

CATHOLIC-ORTHODOX

Q. *What is the difference between the Greek Orthodox and Roman Catholic Churches? What is the procedure for a Roman Catholic to marry a Greek Orthodox in the Greek Orthodox Church—if permissible? Must a Catholic priest be present at the ceremony?*

A. The Greek Orthodox Church is one of a number of Eastern churches which resulted from a split between Eastern and Western Christianity in the 11th century. The causes of this division were certain theological differences, such as the relation of the Holy Spirit to the Father and the Son, and liturgical practices, including the use of leavened versus unleavened bread for the Eucharist, together with the question of the spiritual authority of the Pope. These problems were complicated by political and cultural differences between East and West. Since 1054 the Eastern Church has gone its separate way.

However, of all churches not in union with the Holy See, the Eastern Orthodox are nearest to the Roman Catholic Church in belief. This is why, for example, Roman Catholics are permitted to receive Holy Communion from an Orthodox priest in cases of necessity.

With regard to marriage, it is possible for a Roman Catholic to be married in an Orthodox ceremony with or without the presence of a Roman Catholic priest. It is forbidden to do this without permission from one's local bishop, but even without the permission such a marriage would be considered valid.

Q. *I am a single Catholic and am contemplating marriage with an Orthodox man. He was married for three years in another country. His Church is now in the process of granting him a church divorce. Will the Catholic Church recognize what his church has given him and allow me to be married to him?*

A. I wish I could answer your question. You must present the case to your local bishop. We Roman Catholics are in an ambiguous position in regard to marriages with the Orthodox. Our Church now recognizes as valid a marriage between a Roman Catholic and an Orthodox in an Orthodox church, even without the presence of a Catholic priest. And our Church also recognizes officially that the Orthodox have apostolic succession of orders and the power to make their own church law. In the *Decree on Ecumenism,* Vatican Council II says: "This Sacred Synod solemnly declares that the Churches of the East, while keeping in mind the necessary unity of the whole Church, have the power to govern themselves according to their own disciplines, since these are better suited to the temperament of their faithful and better adapted to foster the good of souls. Although it has not always been honored, the strict observance of this traditional principle is among the prerequisites for any restoration of unity."

To be consistent, therefore, it would seem that our Church must recognize a divorce granted by an Orthodox Church to one of its members. By divorce the Orthodox in many instances mean what our Church calls a declaration of nullity.

But it can also mean a dissolution of the marriage bond in favor of the innocent party in a case of adultery or desertion. The Eastern Church has observed this practice from the earliest days of Christianity. And it is important to note that in the 15th century at the Council of Florence, when the Eastern and Western Churches were briefly reunited, no stipulation was required by the Latin Church that the East give up this practice of divorce.

Q. *I am a girl of 24 in love with a man 27. I'm Catholic; he's Ukrainian Orthodox. I want to get married in my church; he wants to get married in his. We've heard somewhere that both priests could perform the wedding ceremony; so that's not the main problem. What I'd like to know is, what happens when children come? Of course, I want them brought up as Catholics; he wants them to embrace his religion. We are planning to talk to my priest and his, but I first want to know if there is any hope for us to live within our religions. We both know that it will be difficult, but we know we could make it work if there is any way to settle this.*

A. Both priests do not perform the wedding. They may both take part in the ceremony by sharing in the readings, prayers and blessings, but only one may act as the official for both Church and State. The problem of the children is crucial. You won't be able to make a success of your marriage unless you come to some understanding on the religion of the children.

One or the other of you will have to give in. And since his religion is so deeply woven into his cultural and national origins, it is not likely that he will. The promise that you would be expected to make before entering this marriage would be to do all in your power to baptize and raise the children in the Catholic faith. You could honestly make this promise even though you foresaw that he would demand that the children be baptized as Orthodox. You could remain faithful to your own Church, even though the rest of the family was Orthodox. But the chances of this leading to happiness for you are mighty slim. The cards are stacked against you.

CATHOLIC-JEWISH

Q. *Fifteen years ago my only daughter, a good, religious girl, married a Jew, a wonderful and good man. They were married by a justice of the peace, then remarried in a church. From this marriage she has two sons, both raised in the Catholic religion. Both she and the boys have kept up with the Catholic religion. The boys take Communion every Sunday. My daughter has been denied this privilege because she married a Jew.*

Now that we are supposed to love one another even though of different religions, is it permissible for her to get absolution?

A. I fear there has been some misunderstanding here. Your daughter should not have been denied the privilege of receiving the sacraments because she married a Jew. I doubt that this was the reason. If the couple were re-married in a Catholic church, then your daughter would have been reconciled with the Church and permitted to receive Holy Communion. If the remarriage took place in some other Christian church, as seems likely, then your daughter must first rectify her marriage according to the Catholic form of marriage. I suspect that her husband had been previously married and divorced and that is the reason why she cannot receive the sacraments.

Q. *My daughter has fallen in love with a Jewish boy she met in college. S. is a very nice boy and will marry C. in our church. My husband has stated he will not attend the wedding and will disown her. My husband has always been a good Catholic and I can't under-stand this. He reads your column every week. Maybe you can enlighten him.*

A. You flatter you husband by describing him as a good Catholic. He doesn't deserve the name if his opposition to the marriage springs from prejudice against the Jews. His trouble may be ignorance. Perhaps he does not know that Jews are noted for their stable marriages and strong family ties and that marriages between Catholics and Jews can be most successful.

I don't know what to say to your husband other than to remind him that he will be facing another Jew on judgment day.

Q. *If a couple, one Catholic and the other Jewish, who were married by a priest, bring their child up in the*

Jewish faith, will the Catholic be able to go to confession and receive absolution?

A. It all depends on the situation. Obviously, the Jewish partner has gone back on his promises to raise the children as Catholics. He may have decided that the promises were unfairly exacted of him; he may have given in to pressures from his family. We will not judge him.

What has the Catholic partner done? If after serious efforts she finds it impossible to change the situation, she is faced with the choice of seeking a divorce and custody of the child or giving in for the sake of peace and preserving a home where the child can have the love of a father. I should think that the choice would be in favor of keeping the family together, especially in view of the likelihood that the child might resent the decision of the mother as it grew up and came to realize what had happened.

If the Catholic partner did all she could to remain faithful to her promises to raise the child as a Catholic, then she is not guilty of sin for failing. She has nothing to confess on this score. If she was guilty through neglect and indifference and now recognizes her sin, then she does have something to confess. So long as she is determined to do what she can to familiarize the child with Catholicism and to give a lesson in the values of her faith by the way she lives it, there seems to be no reason why she cannot receive the sacraments. She needs them more than others. It would be best for such a person to approach her pastor and explain the situation. To bring up the problem in the confessional first might lead to misunderstanding and an unfortunate refusal.

Q. *We have a daughter who is a practicing Catholic and has no desire to give up her religion. She is engaged to a Jewish boy, and they plan to marry. Can she be married by a rabbi and raise children, should there be any, in the Jewish faith, and still remain a Catholic in the eyes of the Church? She made inquiries of the priest where she made her undergraduate studies, and he tells her that this is proper and can be allowed by the Church. We have made inquiries of our pastor, and he tells us that it is absolutely forbidden and that as a Catholic she must be married by a priest and has the obligation to have any children baptized and brought up in the Catholic Church. Who is right?*

A. Your pastor has not kept up with the changes. Since October 1, 1970, bishops are authorized to dispense from the Catholic form of marriage in individual instances so that a Catholic may be given permission to marry validly in a Protestant, Jewish or civil ceremony. Permission for this must be requested and also a dispensation from the impediment of mixed religion (or in the case of marriage with a Jew from the impediment of disparity of cult).

Before such permission and dispensation are granted, the Catholic party must sign a promise to this effect:

"I reaffirm my faith in Jesus Christ and with God's help intend to continue living that faith in the Catholic Church. I promise to do all that I can to share the faith I have received with our children by having them baptized and reared as Catholics."

The non-Catholic party is not asked to make any kind of promise but must be informed of the kind of promise the Catholic party makes. Note well the nature of the promise: "I promise to do all that I can." This promise could be made by your daughter even though she knows that her husband and family will insist that the children be brought up in the Jewish religion.

Your daughter should insist that she be free to attend Mass and take an active part in her own Church. If she doesn't hold out for this minimum and still wants to think of herself as a Catholic, she will lose all respect for herself and more than likely soon develop a deep resentment against her husband. The one hope she has of making a success of this marriage is to hold out for her minimum. By the way she subsequently lives, by the way she shows what a Christian mother and wife can be, she may eventually win some or all of the children to her faith. Thus she will be fulfilling her promise to do all she can.

It is possible, therefore, for your daughter to marry the Jewish man on his demands, providing he is willing to go with her to her priest, take the required instructions and let her obtain permission for a Jewish wedding to count as valid. If he is not willing to do this much for her, then he does not love her and there is nothing but trouble and misery ahead for both of them.

Q. *My niece is going out with a Jewish boy. They would get married in a Catholic church, but he would not agree to have the children baptized. If that would happen would my niece be excommunicated from the Church? The young man said he would rather see his children pick their own religion, be it the Catholic faith or the Jewish, whichever they choose.*

A. No, your niece would not be excommunicated if she married the Jewish man under his conditions. According to the latest church law, the party who is not a Catholic is not obliged to make promises to raise the children in the Catholic faith, as used to be the case. The Catholic must promise to remain faithful to his Church and to do all in his power to have the childen baptized and raised as Catholics, and the non-Catholic must be informed of this promise, before permission for a marriage in the Church is granted.

However, no certainty is required that the children be brought up as Catholics. The sincere convictions of the non-Catholic parent must be considered and respected. It may happen that the best efforts of the Catholic parent may not prevail because the other party is equally determined the children be raised in another faith. This is far from an ideal situation, and a couple that foresees conflict over the religion of their children should be urged to reach an agreement before marriage and if this is not possible should be dissuaded from marriage.

Before the new regulations, when the non-Catholic party refused to promise not to oppose the Catholic rearing of the children, the case sometimes was referred to Rome. The Holy See usually permitted the marriage provided there was no prior agreement that excluded the possibility of rearing the children in the Catholic faith. (Cf. *The Church Under Tension* by Alcuin Coyle and Dismas Bonner, Catholic Book Publishing Co., N.Y. 1972.) An agreement to let the children decide would not by any means exclude the possibility of rearing the children in the Catholic faith or keep the Catholic party from doing all within her power to bring this about.

Q. *I am contemplating a marriage with a divorced Jew who married a Jewess in his own religion. I would like to know if the Catholic Church would consider this marriage valid as I would like to marry in the Catholic Church.*

A. The Jews take marriage seriously. The presumption, certainly, is that the man's marriage was valid, and you would not be allowed to marry him in the Catholic Church. Of course, there could have been something in the way that made the marriage invalid. You should discuss the possibilities with your parish priest.

Q. *In a recent column, you answered a question about a Catholic marrying a Jew who had previously contracted a marriage with another Jew. You said: "The presumption, certainly, is that the man's marriage was valid, and you would not be allowed to marry him in the Catholic Church." It seems to me that you neglect the important fact of the so-called Pauline Privilege. The Church can and does dissolve such nonsacramental marriages. Since great harm may be done to souls, I think the matter should be corrected (assuming I'm correct).*

A. You are correct. If the Jewish man is willing to be baptized and enter the Church and his divorced wife will not accept him back and agree to live in peace with a Christian, he may be given permission to use the Pauline Privilege. This means that in favor of his new faith he is permitted to enter marriage with a Christian, and the previous marriage is dissolved at the moment he contracts the new. The first marriage between two persons not baptized is not a sacramental Christian marriage. Such a marriage, the Church teaches, can be dissolved in favor of the faith.

It is the exceptional Jew who becomes a Christian to marry. I hesitated to suggest this remote possibility to the girl who wondered whether there was any hope of marriage with a divorced Jew.

MARRIAGE OUTSIDE THE CHURCH

Q. *In a recent column you told a Catholic woman that her civil marriage did not excommunicate her. I must admit to being ignorant as to why not. I was under the impression that any marriage of a civil nature not followed by a church ceremony carried with it this penalty. Will you explain?*

A. Marriages of Catholics contracted before a civil magistrate have never been cause for excommunication. They are not valid in the eyes of the Church and a person is considered living in a state of sin until such a marriage is rectified by the Church or dissolved, but the penalty of excommunication is not incurred. Previously, Catholics who were married before a minister of another religion incurred excommunication but now even in this case the penalty no longer applies.

Your confusion arises, perhaps, from an inadequate understanding of the penalty of excommunication. And it is not surprising that your understanding is inadequate, for excommunication no longer has much meaning in the society in which we live. Those who are excommunicated are officially cut off from membership in the Church. In the days when everybody in a community belonged to the Church, the penalty of excommunication could lead to ostracism. It could be an extreme punishment meant to keep people in line. Persons who were excommunicated had to have the penalty removed by a bishop.

Q. *I have a troubled soul. I am a Catholic who married outside the Church in a civil wedding. I ran my home as any Catholic mother would, sent my children to Catholic school and the sacraments. I was denied the privileges of the sacraments, but I never lost my love for God. Now I am a widow. How do I start to live with God again?*

A. You are living with him now. God never left you. That is why you brought your children up in the faith, that is why you never lost the faith and sense the need of him now.

Why make difficult what is so easy? Go to confession to any priest. Tell him you were married in a civil ceremony 25 years ago, that you are now a widow and then say: "Please help me." He'll ask you questions that will assist you in making a good confession and give you absolution immediately. Your civil marriage did not excommunicate you.

Q. *Is it possible for a Catholic couple who were married by a justice of the peace to have their marriage blessed by the Catholic Church if they are practicing birth control? The couple have two children.*

A. Yes, it is possible. Perhaps once you are married properly and aided by the sacrament of Matrimony you will be surer that whatever decision you make regarding children will be made generously and responsibly.

Q. *My son at 19 years of age married a girl of 16 be-*

fore a judge. It lasted three months and is now being dissolved. Recently during the funeral Mass for one of his grandparents the family received Communion as a group. I cautioned him that he could not receive Communion. I've been wondering if I was wrong or right. Where does someone in his situation stand in the Church?

A. If his marriage is being dissolved, your son presumably no longer lives with the girl. He is free, therefore, to return to the sacraments. Advise him to get to confession. The marriage before the judge is not considered valid by the Church; so your son is free to marry in the Church once the civil divorce or annulment is granted. When the time comes for a serious marriage, he will need a declaration of the nullity of this civil marriage from church authorities.

Q. I am a widow in my 50's planning to get married again to a single man the same age. He's not baptized although he attended Sunday school in his youth. From what I gather, he fears marriage. He has common law in mind, which I ruled out. He suggested the justice of the peace, but that I wouldn't agree to either.

I've always stayed with the Church. I wonder if I would commit a grave sin by getting married by a Protestant minister with the understanding we would have the marriage rectified in the Catholic Church later. It would make him feel better. I know with just a tiny obstacle in the road, he'll back out.

A. A man in his 50's who has never married is a poor gamble as a marriage partner. He is used to living alone and not accustomed to thinking of the needs and wishes of others. He may, therefore, be inconsiderate and selfish. This is not true, of course, of all long-term bachelors, but your man gives every indication of the worst.

He is afraid of marriage. He wants you on his own terms. Wake up. Unless he is willing to marry you on your terms, drop him like a hot potato. If a "tiny obstacle" will induce him to back out, he's not worth having. He's certainly not worth committing sin to get. And, yes, what you are contemplating is gravely sinful.

Q. *I am getting married out of the Church due to the fact that my fiancee is divorced. We have already discussed the matter with my parish priest. I was told I could not receive the sacraments. I originally accepted this, but now I am wondering what would happen if I continued to receive the sacraments anyway. I don't believe I am doing anything wrong and I can't help wondering if God would make these restrictions if he were here. From my standpoint, this is entirely a Church law and not one God made. Why does the Church tell people what they can and can't do? Please give me some concrete thoughts to make this situation easier. I'm deeply in love and I'm going to get married regardless. I just happen to be one of those people who are very sensitive and worry a lot.*

A. Since you have already made up your mind, there seems to be nothing I can say that will keep you from taking a step you may regret for years to come. You are struggling now to justify what you are about to do. I predict that, sensitive as you are, you will continue to anguish over your situation after you have married outside the Church.

You wouldn't be human if you didn't try to justify your actions, and it is inevitable for persons in your dilemma to blame conservative, old celibate popes and bishops for their predicament. I suspect those are the people you have in mind when you think of the Church as telling you what you can and cannot do. But the pope and bishops are merely the spokesmen of the whole Church; they remind us of what our ancestors believed came down from Christ; and were the pope suddenly to announce that from now on the Catholic Church would permit anyone to marry no matter how or why divorced, there would be an immediate and vociferous reaction from great hordes of the faithful.

The clergy, from the pope on down, are not insensitive to your problem. The hardest thing a parish priest has to do is to tell people in your situation that he cannot help them. He is torn between his desire to help someone with a problem of conscience and the duty to uphold a Christian concept of marriage and family life that he believes to be God's plan for right living.

My advice to you, if you must do what you are determined to do, is to admit you find it impossible to live up to the Christian ideal of marriage, throw yourself on the mercy of God and pray that you keep the faith, raise your children in the Church, and remain as active a member of it as your condition allows. You can still attend Mass, even though not permitted to partake of Communion. Countless others have done this and successfully have passed the faith on to their children. So God must have his own way of getting around the restrictions he places on his Church.

There is a growing demand within the Church today to allow Catholics whose marriages are considered invalid to receive the sacraments. As matters stand now, murderers, embezzlers, any sinners — you name them — can repent and return to the sacraments, but one who marries outside the Church cannot be reconciled. The problem is that a Catholic in an invalid marriage is not considered repentant until he gets out of the marriage. But is this fair? If the marriage is stable and successful, the Catholic would seem to be obliged to remain in it for the sake of the spouse and children. A thief who wants to restore the money he stole is considered repentant even though there is no possibility of returning it. Why cannot a Catholic unable to get out of a marriage situation be considered repentant? In some cases it would seem that such Catholics should be allowed to receive the sacraments, and indeed some confessors are permitting this. You, of course, are not in such a situation, but someday you may be.

Q. *Some months ago my daughter got married by a justice of the peace. Her husband has no religion, but my daughter misses her own, and would like to go to confession and Communion. I asked the priest, and he said she must first right her marriage. If her husband does not wish to repeat marriage vows, does this mean she cannot ever receive the sacraments?*

A. Your daughter should talk the problem over with a priest. It is possible that when her husband understands what is wanted and why, he will be willing to renew his vows before a priest. If he refuses to do this but still gives evidence that he wants his marriage with your daughter to be permanent, then the priest may apply to the bishop for what is known as a sanation of the marriage. This means that the bishop dispenses from the Catholic form of marriage and declares the union of your daughter and her husband to be valid from the very beginning. As far as the Church laws are concerned, then, this is a binding, Catholic marriage, and your daughter is in good standing with the Church.

Three things must be present before this sanation can be granted: 1) the unwillingness of the non-Catholic party to renew the vows before a priest; 2) there must have been true matrimonial consent in the beginning and this must persevere; 3) the Catholic party must be willing to do everything possible to bring up the children in the Church. It is not necessary that the non-Catholic party know about the granting of the sanation.

Q. *My wife, a Catholic, was married twice in civil ceremonies, in both instances to Protestants, one approximately 28 years ago and the other about 22 years ago. I also am Catholic. I married my wife almost 20 years ago. I know that this automatically excommunicated us. Our children have all had a Catholic education. I am given to understand the Church regards these marriages as still lawful and that I cannot marry in the Church until the law is changed. I would like to know if this is still the Church policy.*

A. There has been no change in policy, but if I understand you rightly you don't need a change and are free to have your present union rectified by the Church. If your wife's two previous marriages were before a justice of the peace and never rectified before a priest and she was a Catholic at the time she married, then she is free to marry according to the laws of the Church. Go see your parish priest. I just can't believe you were never told this before. Are you sure of your facts?

MARRIAGES REQUIRING DISPENSATIONS

Q. *I have a son who is dating a girl who is his second cousin. It's getting more serious as it goes along. Her father is a first cousin to his father. Also her mother is a first cousin to his mother. Could he marry her?*

A. The couple would need a dispensation from the minor impediment of consanguinity. Dispensations for second cousins are readily granted. The fact that there is a double relationship would make no difference.

Q. *The report is being circulated that as of October 1, 1970, all marriages in which a Catholic is involved that take place before a justice of the peace or Protestant minister are considered as valid by the Church. Could this be true?*

A. The report is not accurate. From October 1, 1970, new regulations permit bishops to dispense Catholics for serious reasons from the obligation of the Catholic form of marriage so that they may validly be married to a member of some other religion in a non-Catholic ceremony. The ceremony need not be religious, but it must be some public form of ceremony. Without such a dispensation the marriage would not be considered valid by the Catholic Church.

The purpose of this change is to promote better understanding between the churches and pave the way for church unity. Reasons for granting the dispensation would, therefore, have to do with helping a young couple get off to a better start in a mixed marriage. In cases where the bride is Protestant, frequently her parents feel the marriage ought to take place in their church. Now this can be possible. Or there are times when the only compromise would be a marriage before a judge. In the past these were invalid; now with the dispensation they can be valid.

Q. *My daughter has become engaged to a young man who has no religion at all. In fact, his parents do not practice any religion. Can such a marriage take place in the Church and will she have the privilege of the Mass?*

You have written about Catholics marrying baptized Protestants, but what about my daughter's case?

A. The conditions which you describe are fairly common in so-called Catholic countries. There marriages between Catholics and other baptized Christians are infrequent. Most often the non-Catholic party has no religious affiliation or background whatsoever.

If your daughter wishes to marry in the Church she must receive a dispensation. She may be able to have a nuptial Mass, depending on her diocese's ruling in the matter. Your pastor will be able to answer her questions and initiate the necessary procedures.

Q. *My girl friend lost her husband about a year ago. Lately she has been keeping company with his brother, who isn't married. They are getting quite fond of each*

other. I told her she shouldn't get too serious, as mar-
riage wouldn't be possible with her own brother-in-law.
But she claims they can be married, that the Church
laws are so lenient now that such a marriage is pos-
sible. It she right or am I?

A. You are both partly right and partly wrong. The
Church does have an impediment against marriages between in-laws, but she does dispense from this impediment. Your girl friend can marry her brother-in-law if
they obtain the proper dispensation from their bishop.
But this is not because the laws have been relaxed. This
was possible long before the modern changes.

Q. *Are the "Six Precepts of the Church" still in effect?*
I would like information on No. 6, which says: "Not to
marry persons within the third degree of kindred."
May a couple marry if the boy's grandmother and the
girl's grandfather are brother and sister and what about
a couple whose grandparents are first cousins?

A. There are far more than six laws of the Church.
They were summarized and codified in 1918 into 2414
canons. The so-called "Six Precepts of the Church" were
a catechism summary of the laws that affect most often
the majority of the members of the Church.

Church law still does forbid marriages between persons related within the third degree of kindred. Brothers
and sisters are related in the first degree; first cousins in
the second; and second cousins in the third degree.

If the grandparents are first cousins, then the couple
would be third cousins or related in the fourth degree;
they are free to marry. If the grandparents are brother

and sister, then the couple would be second cousins, or related in the third degree. They could marry, however, with a dispensation which is readily granted.

Q. *Can I be granted a dispensation to marry a person who does not attend any church and has never been baptized? My boyfriend is quite willing to bring our children up as Catholics.*

A. Of course you may. No problem here at all. You need a dispensation from the church impediment of disparity of cult, as distinguished from a dispensation from the impediment of mixed religion which you would need to marry a baptized member of some other Christian church. The one is as readily granted today as the other.

Q. *A while back I read in your column that second cousins had to get a dispensation to get married. My husband and I are second cousins, and we have been married for 28 years. At the time of our wedding I asked my husband if he told the priest that we were related, and he told me "yes," but after reading your answer and knowing my husband as well as I know him now, I know he never mentioned it.*

What effect does this have on our marriage? Should we do something about it? Is our marriage valid as a sacrament? We do not get along at all, and it seems no matter how hard I pray or work at making our marriage work, it's all to no avail. But I can't believe that the lack of a dispensation would keep God from answering my prayers and effort.

A. Whether or not a dispensation was granted, you and

your husband undoubtedly thought you were living in a valid marriage. Sacrament or not, valid or not, God would not have withheld from you the graces you needed for your life together. If you are not getting along, there must be other reasons than the failure of God to listen.

If your marriage were invalid for lack of the proper dispensation, it would be what is known according to church law as a putative marriage. This would mean that all children born of the union are considered legitimate according to church law.

If you have serious doubts about whether or not a dispensation was granted, you may settle them by inquiring for information at the church where you were married. On the marriage record it should state whether or not a dispensation was granted. The priest who assisted at your marriage should have asked you as well as your husband about any possible relationship. It is quite possible that if he knew your families well he may have been aware of the impediment and applied for the dispensation without your knowledge.

Should you discover that no dispensation was granted and you are, indeed, second cousins, you should ask your pastor to obtain a dispensation and repeat your vows before him. This might give you a fresh start in your married life. If, however, the marriage is hopeless, and you see a divorce in the future, it would seem best to separate and ask the Church for a declaration of nullity.

Q. *My son wants a Baptist minister to marry him to a Baptist girl in her church. Can he get a dispensation from his pastor provided he promises to have his children baptized in the Catholic Church?*

A. Yes. He must obtain a special dispensation from his bishop through his parish priest. The promise he makes is to do all he can to raise his children as Catholics.

Q. *Are two young people whose fathers are first cousins too closely related to marry? My son is very interested in the girl.*

A. These two are second cousins, related in the third degree of the collateral line as the Church reckons it (the direct line is father-daughter-grandson). The Church does have an impediment of consanguinity that forbids marriage between blood relations of the third degree. However, dispensations from this impediment are granted without difficulty. If the couple is serious, they should talk to a priest about the possibility of a dispensation, which can be granted by the local bishop.

Q. *Is a Catholic married in the eyes of the Catholic faith if he marries in another ceremony by an authorized person of another faith without a priest present?*

A. If no dispensation from the form of Catholic marriage has been obtained, they are not considered married in the eyes of the Catholic Church. However, today a Catholic may be married before a Protestant minister, a Jewish rabbi, or even a justice of the peace, without a priest present, if the proper dispensation is obtained from a bishop.

Q. *If a man's wife passed away about three years ago, is it permissible to marry his deceased wife's sister who has never been married and both live up to the Catholic Church's teaching?*

A. There is a major impediment of affinity in the first degree to such a marriage. For serious reasons the local bishop can dispense from this impediment. A case like this should be submitted to the bishop through the pastor.

Q. *Some time ago you answered a question from a man who wanted to know if it is legal to marry his deceased wife's sister. You answered in the negative using a bunch of fifty-dollar words and beat around the bush with really a vague answer. Why didn't you elaborate a little bit, as you have a way of doing with so many other questions? Just what is this "major impediment of affinity in the first degree" that could preclude a legal marriage? Why are you so secretive about this and other potentially controversial issues?*

A. I am sorry I did not realize that the problem was so difficult. I did clearly say that "for serious reasons the local bishop can dispense from the impediment." This means that a Catholic man could marry his sister-in-law. I myself have obtained this dispensation several times so that a man who lost his wife might have a mother for his children by marrying their aunt, the sister of his wife. The impediment of affinity is not just a church law. A good number of states of the U. S. have affinity laws. It is a bit unusual to marry your sister-in-law, or your mother-in-law or your stepdaughter, isn't it?

If we take seriously the biblical teaching that man and wife become two in one flesh, then they become related in some sense to the kin of the other party. People of all nations have recognized this. Today in our modern civilizations, when families are not as close as they used to be, perhaps the laws concerning affinity are not so necessary. Therefore, the Church is much more willing to dispense from them today. What's the big problem? How many men or women do you know who are married to their brother- or sister-in-law?

Q. *Recently you stated, in effect, that the Catholic Church considers the marriage of a Catholic by a justice of the peace as valid if the proper dispensation is obtained. Please explain, because in the past a Catholic married by anyone other than a duly ordained priest or minister was living in sin.*

A. According to our Church law, a Catholic is obliged to be married before an authorized priest and two witnesses — not just duly ordained, but authorized, either as priest in charge of the place where the marriage takes place or authorized by him.

This is a necessary requirement for a marriage to be considered valid by the Church, and one not so married, whether before a duly ordained minister or justice of the peace is considered, as you put it, living in sin. This requirement does not apply to Protestants or other non-Catholics but affects Catholics only, or non-Catholics when they marry Catholics. Therefore two Protestants married before a justice of the peace are considered validly married.

The Catholic Church did not and does not consider a marriage of a Catholic before a Protestant minister as valid unless a dispensation from the required Catholic form of marriage is obtained. This dispensation is something new. When it is granted by a bishop, he specifies that a given Catholic is dispensed so that he/she may be validly married to a given non-Catholic party before a specified Protestant minister, Jewish rabbi or even a justice of the peace, if there is a good reason for this. It is possible that neither family is willing to take part in a marriage in the church or synagogue of the other and a judge or justice of the peace would be a compromise.

May I point out two things about this new dispensation? The marriage even though it is performed in a Protestant church is duly entered in the marriage records of the parish church of the Catholic party. And for the validity of the marriage it is not necessary that a priest be present to share in the ceremony.

part 3

Married Life

Married Life

THE MARRIED COUPLE

Q. *According to the Apostle Paul's teaching is not the husband the head of the family? Did he ever say that marriage is a 50-50 proposition?*

A. You must have in mind Paul's statement on marriage in Ephesians, part of which states: "Wives be subject to your husbands as to the Lord" (Eph 5:22). If we wanted to play a game of scriptural roulette, which used to be quite popular in theological discussions, we could spin over to Galatians and answer that Paul also said: "There is neither Jew nor Greek, there is neither slave nor free, there is neither male nor female; for you are all one in Christ Jesus" (Gal 3:28). Score a point for equality. But let's be a little more serious about this.

In the passage from Ephesians, St. Paul is speaking out of the particular culture in which he and his readers lived. Women in those days lived perpetually under the guardianship of a man, a father in the case of young or unmarried women, or a husband in the case of married women. This was a situation Paul and his contemporaries took for granted; he wisely adapted his teaching to fit a particular social structure. In effect, he is saying that wives should live out their existing situation in a Christian manner. He gives the same advice to slaves a few verses later.

When Paul is dealing with the core of the Christian message, stripped of social and cultural considerations, as he does in the passage from Galatians, he does not hesitate to proclaim the equality of all men in the life they share in Christ.

The cultural, social structures, customs and attitudes Paul was familiar with were all un-Christian. He could not possibly foresee what a Christian culture and social structure would become once the glorious doctrines of the freedom of Christ, the dignity and equality of men he himself preached had fermented in society.

It took a long time before Christians recognized that slavery was utterly at odds with Christian belief. And the ladies, I wouldn't be surprised, feel that the status of women is still partly at odds with a mature Christian conception of the dignity of man. They should take heart from the encouraging words of Vatican Council's *Constitution on the Church in the Modern World:*

"The intimate partnership of married life and love has been established by the Creator and qualified by his laws and is rooted in the conjugal covenant of irrevocable personal consent. . . . Firmly established by the Lord, the unity of marriage will radiate from the equal personal dignity of wife and husband, a dignity acknowledged by mutual and total love."

This comes close to putting approval on the present-day approach to marriage as a 50-50 proposition.

Irate husbands are kindly asked to moderate their language when they respond to this effort.

Q. *I am a woman of 29 years with three children, one of whom is retarded. I am unhappily married to a man who has neither time for me nor my children, shirks responsibility and objects to my being a convert to the Catholic Church.*

My problem is this: I have been fighting a terrible attraction to another man. I have been writing to him. I realize I am wrong. But I am in dire need of some suggestions as this battle with myself has been going on too long.

A. At the risk of playing amateur psychologist, let me offer a few general observations about your situation.

You are unhappy in your marriage because where you expected to find comfort, understanding and love you are experiencing opposition and neglect. You see in the other man a promise of what you expected from married life in the first place. And more than likely you seek something else from him. If you are like everyone else, you have a strong urge to be recognized, to feel important. When this essential part of our human equipment is frustrated, when we are made to feel that we are not important, when the good in us is not recognized, then we either give up and fall into a kind of dull, listless, unproductive existence or else we try to get into another situation where we can be recognized and feel important.

Your husband by his criticism, opposition and neglect is constantly deflating your ego. Much of the attraction of the other man, therefore, may be the need you have to be appreciated, to be made important.

What to do about the problem? There are three answers right in your home. Your children. As far as they are concerned you are the most important person in the world. You are especially important, of course, to your retarded child. There are a lot of women in this world who would give anything to have what you have to make life worthwhile.

If you concentrate on your position as mother, convince yourself of the importance of your job in raising your children, in short, if you can accept what is, rather than dreaming of what might be, then you would be more at peace with yourself and others, then the attraction to what you know is wrong would not be so strong. This is not an easy thing to do, but your new faith, if you understand it properly, should lead you to love the only other man who can make it possible — Jesus Christ.

Q. *I have a problem that may sound silly. When I first dated my husband, I wasn't very settled down, being only 16, so I kept breaking up with him. Some other girl fell in love with him. I'm sure he wasn't in love with her but I think he delighted in the idea that she was in love with him. It just made me feel like my love wasn't enough for him. Every time we went to a certain place, she was usually there and he would always dance with her. He said he just felt sorry for her. I think maybe he wanted to hurt me because I had hurt him, but I'm so mixed up that I don't know what I think.*

She is married now, too. Her husband runs around on her. Now I feel like he thinks, "Boy, she would have had it nice if she could have married me." I'm not sure how I feel about all this or maybe I would be okay. I

*used to talk to my husband about it, but I can't any-
more. I think he's fed up with it. This all happened
eight years ago. We've gotten married since and have
children, and this is still on my mind all the time. My
husband is the most important thing in my life and if I
can't get this straightened out I don't think I will ever
be happy.*

A. You should get busy and look for people around you
who have real problems. Count your blessings for a
change. And stop torturing yourself needlessly. Deep
down you may feel that you are not being the perfect
wife. But who is perfect?

Your husband must be happy with you in your marriage because if what you say is true, that you live only
for him, he can't help but realize this. Don't ever bring
up the subject of the other girl again. When you think
of her, use this as a stimulus to be a better wife. Your
husband seems to have forgotten the past. You should
too.

Q. *Is there something in the male species that feels
desperate at times because of working conditions or
outside pressure that necessitates him being surly, insulting and negative to his spouse when truly the
spouse does all she can to make his home and hearth
comfortable, loving and friendly? Could it be that the
ones who love him are the last chance for him to feed
his ego, even though insulting them seems necessary
at the time? If so, isn't there always the chance of the
"last straw breaking the camel's back"?*

A. It could be, and there is the chance. Tell him so.

But try harder at building up his ego in a friendly, loving way and seek to find out what the outside pressures might be.

Q. *You wrote recently about "exclusive possession of one another" in marriage. Religion and society do not seem to recognize that it is possible to have more than one love in a lifetime—that love for another can and does happen while being happily married.*

In my case, I broke off the association with the man I was falling in love with and, it seems, transferred or extended that much more love to my husband. This has helped somewhat, but it has been months since I have seen this man, and I still cannot forget or stop loving him.

Don't you think there is room for improvement in marriage laws? What is wrong with loving more than one man (or woman)?

A. You make me think of Victor Herbert's "Everyday Is Ladies' Day with Me," and the man who wouldn't marry because he wanted to love them all.

I thing you have really answered yourself. The man is still bugging you. Put him out of your mind. You have been lucky so far. Don't push your luck.

Friendship with other men is something else again. There are times when married persons need the advice and support of friends of the opposite sex, to help understand their spouse and sometimes to save their marriage. A couple needs lots of friends, if for no other reason than to keep their love for each other from becoming too possessive. Or so it seems to me. But what do I know about it?

Q. *If a marriage between two Catholics fails because of parental interference, is it possible to have such a marriage dissolved?*

A. If two Catholics marry properly and live together as man and wife, the Church does not dissolve the marriage. The Church can declare that such a marriage was null and void from the beginning if there was some invalidating impediment in the way.

Parental influence would not directly invalidate a marriage. There is, however, a possibility that excessive parental influence could mean that one of the parties was forced into marriage by the parents or that one was so dominated by the parents that he or she was not mature enough to contract a permanent marriage. Questions like this should be submitted to your parish priest, for it is only by personal questioning that you can be helped to explain your case clearly.

Q. *I have been married for 29 years to a good Protestant man. Our three children were raised as Catholics, all attending Catholic schools. When my mother died 26 years ago my dad came to live with us and did until his death this year. Through all these years my husband has gone to Mass with me sometimes, off and on. He never attended his own church (Lutheran) since the day we married.*

At the funeral Mass for my dad, my husband really surprised me by receiving Holy Communion. He felt it would make me happy and also did it for my father. An aunt of mine says he was very definitely wrong. Was he really wrong, was his act sacrilegious?

A. It is obvious that your husband thought he was doing something good. He certainly had no intentions of being disrespectful. Therefore, what he did was not wrong for him and surely was not sacrilegious. But there was more to his action than this, I think. Brought up as a Lutheran and the father of a Catholic family, your husband had a good understanding of what the Eucharist means. He was trying to show his unity with you at such a solemn moment. I hope you thanked him. And I wonder whether you invited him to join you regularly at Communion by becoming a full-fledged member of the Church. He probably knows enough already to be admitted with very little preparation. Many men in your husband's situation hesitate to make the step because they are held back by the prospect of a long course of instructions.

What your husband did happens more and more often these days. Maybe the Holy Spirit is trying to tell us something. I said once before that I hope our Church soon permits the Protestant spouse to receive Communion on special family occasions, such as First Communion, weddings and funerals.

Q. *A dear friend of mine married a young man back from Vietnam. Unfortunately he now drinks, gambles and even beats her. Why did God allow this to happen? She's a good girl. Why is she being punished?*

A. I don't know. She'll have to wait for God's answer. The story of Joseph in the Book of Genesis may help here. Joseph must have wondered why God permitted his brothers to sell him into slavery to the Egyptians. But years later, when his brothers came to Egypt seeking food during the famine, he was able to tell them: "Do not reproach yourselves for having sold me here. It was really for the sake of saving lives that God sent me here ahead of you" (Gn 45:5). The bible is full of lessons like this of how God turns the evil of men into good.

Q. *I'm 45 years old and lonely. My husband and I were both raised Catholic. We brought children into the world and now they are about raised. I read a lot and enjoy keeping up on the latest issues of the day. I would have loved to travel, but my husband traveled in World War II and never wanted to take a vacation. He always had two jobs as a young husband and was home only to sleep. He never enjoyed me or the children. He enjoyed everything and everyone but us. Now we have nothing in common. He works out of town, as he couldn't find work at home. He really doesn't bother much with us. What does the future hold for me and many Catholics like me?*

A. I'm passing the buck on this one and asking the readers to help. Your problem is by no means unique. Others have faced it and maybe found a solution other than divorce. Any help is welcome.

I have much empathy and great sympathy for the woman who has nothing in common with the husband who has no use for her, and doesn't know what to do with herself now that her children are about raised. I went down that road myself and I'd like to tell her a thing or two:

Stop being sorry for yourself. You are 45 years old; half your life is ahead of you. Admit to yourself that part of the breakdown of your marriage is your own doing, or undoing, and cannot be done over. But what you do from now on can bring changes.

You have a legal claim on your husband. Keep it and use it, not as a bind but as a structure in which to build another and better life. This will be slow, but if you work diligently and with that one idea in mind, you'll be so busy that time will speed. Get out of the house, which you indicate is not a home, and see the world in your own neighborhood, city and state. You'll like your house better. Find a job—either for money or for charity—to fill your days and nights if your husband is away much of the time.

Your husband must come home sometime. Talk and talk—about what you have been doing, even though he seems not to listen or be interested. Some of what you say will rub off and sink in. In your telling, weave in hints of how you feel. Don't accuse or complain about his lack of interest.

A. A surprising number of people took up the "buck" I passed and sent advice to the woman whose husband held two jobs as a young father and enjoyed everything and everyone but wife and children. They were all women, and they were all of one mind. Here are two more samples:

"Seems to me she needs to do a bit of soul searching. Is she really trying to make a reasonably happy life for herself in her circumstances or has she decided she wants a divorce and is looking for someone to justify it for her?

"She should pursue her husband and try to win him back. Apparently he was bored at home. I wonder why the lady didn't follow her husband when his employment was changed to 'out of town.' She lists her own interests but doesn't mention the things that her husband enjoys. Maybe she should try to find out some of these things and try to participate to some extent.

"We all like a little praise for our efforts once in a while. She should praise him occasionally for working so hard in the past and at the present, act glad to see him when he comes home, compliment his maturing good looks, plan something extra just for him once in a while; never nag or harp on a subject, find something nice to say about him to the children, and don't be too demanding for worldly possessions.

"Someone gave me this advice several years ago and it sure did work. Sometimes we have to reach out to another person first. She should try it; she might like it."

I can identify with the woman whose husband won't have anything to do with her and who is lonely because her children are about to leave her. I've "been there." The answer boils down to the fact that this 45-year-old is not just a woman, nor a wife, nor a mother, nor a housewife, nor a Catholic. She is a person, a child of God, an individual, whole and complete in and of herself. Marriage is not so much a relationship as a way of life. (Oh, yes, I too would like for it to be a relationship, but the simple fact of the matter is that it is not and we live happier, healthier lives if we face and accept reality.)

Motherhood is a job, a career, and a very large and serious responsibility. But anyone who is able to think at all knows that children grow up and that when they do they must leave home. Parents should be able to see this coming and prepare themselves as well as their children for the happy event. But too many women wrap themselves up completely in being mothers and homemakers, and when that job comes to an end they are lost—so lost that many of them fall apart, physically, mentally, emotionally and spiritually.

The alternative is not to build your life around your husband, because he, too, may leave you, either by dying or by living in his own little private world from which you and the children are excluded. It has been my experience and observation that very few men really "get married," by which I mean few men become husbands, fathers, heads of households, etc. They are too busy pursuing their own dreams and aspirations, and home is just a place to return to for food, sleep, clean clothes and sexual gratification. If you made the mistake of choosing one of these nonhusband-nonfather types, the answer is not to blame him, not to resent him, not to blame yourself, and above all, not to quit living and wallow in self-pity for the rest of your days. You may have made a mistake, but you can't undo what is done. You put the past behind you and go forward. Now you are free to get acquainted with yourself, to find out who you are, what you are, why you are here, and what you can do. In short, Mommy, the time has come for you to start growing up, become a whole, mature, integrated human being. Stop pondering your needs and wants and start pondering what you have to give.

A. Thanks for a different approach to the problem. But now we are in trouble with the men.

Q. *I have been married for three years to a very fine man. At the time of our marriage I became Catholic. He is a lifelong Catholic. We began going to a "liberal church" soon after we were married. It is too liberal for me. Confession is not held or ever even mentioned and the holy days usually are not observed. I realize that most churches are not this liberal in their modern liturgy; this one is. We have been attending for three years, and I dread going. He refuses to attend anywhere else. Should I attend and shut up? I am afraid if I complain he may not attend anywhere. I am tolerant enough to realize these people have a right to do their own thing but what should I do?*

A. I think I'd attend and shut up, if I were you. You can visit another church for confession or a weekday Mass that is more to your liking. In these days of change and experiment in the Church we all must put into practice the policy of live and let live and trust that the Holy Spirit will see us through the storm.

Q. *I have been married over 25 years, have a nice family, but my marriage is "dead." My husband has abused me both physically and mentally, and there are times I know not if I can stand on two feet and make it. Have had therapy sessions (he wouldn't go) etc. My problem is that even though I have children in grade school that need me, I want to pray for death. Is it seriously wrong to pray for death when life is so unbearable?*

A. In the mental turmoil you are experiencing you would not be guilty of serious sin if you prayed for death.

But this would be giving up, and the one thing you must not do is stop hoping that God will give you the strength you need to survive and that some therapist or psychiatrist can help you.

Pray for the strength to carry on. Your children need you, for if your husband is so selfish that he is not willing to help you face your problems by cooperating with your therapist, he cannot be much of a father. Your husband, unfortunately, is like many other marriage partners who are largely responsible for the mental problems of their spouses and refuse to admit they themselves need counseling. Keep on seeking for competent medical help and someone who can convince your husband that he must cooperate.

Q. *My wife and I are both Catholics. She now wants to leave the Roman Catholic Church because she no longer believes in the doctrines of the Roman Catholic Church but believes the doctrines of the bible. We have been married for 35 years. Our doctrinal beliefs do not coincide, and I feel that I cannot live with her as her husband under the same roof. She is a good woman, but she does not want to remain a Roman Catholic.*

A. If she is a good woman, then you as a Catholic should continue to live with her and be faithful to your marriage vows. Be kind to her and inspire her by the way you live to recognize that your own faith helps you to be a good husband. Your wife never knew much about her Roman Catholic faith if she does not know that the Roman Catholic Church bases her doctrines upon the bible. So, what she is leaving is not the Catholic

Church but what she thought was the Catholic Church. Be charitable and presume she is in good faith.

Q. *Is a married woman guilty of mortal sin if she masturbates? I have a problem reaching a climax through intercourse on occasion. It's a week since this happened and my husband has made no attempt at intercourse. I just cannot deal with the tension this arouses. There are a lot of problems with him, the children and myself that I am trying to resolve. I am in therapy, but I cannot bring this up with the therapist or my husband. Please advise.*

A. Yours is a delicate question which I hesitate to answer in the religious press. But in a day when youngsters can read all about matters such as this in the morning newspaper, I feel that our people need to have an answer from a religious and moral point of view.

Moral theologians have long taught that it is not sinful for a woman to help herself to a climax after intercourse. You should discuss your problem honestly and openly with your husband. Much of your trouble may come from lack of communication with him. You should make known to your therapist this difficulty. He or she may be able to bring the two of you together and thrash out the problem.

Satisfaction apart from union with your husband could be sinful, but in your case because of the tensions and difficulties you are experiencing, the guilt would be greatly diminished and not likely to be serious. Your principal mistake might very well be a refusal to get help from your therapist and husband so that you can remove the occasion of sin.

One of the principal purposes of sex is to promote love between husband and wife, to relieve tensions and create an atmosphere of peace and harmony where children can sense security and love. Your failure to realize this may be the cause of your problems with yourself and your children. I recommend you talk this whole matter over with a sympathetic priest. You won't shock him or tell him something he hasn't heard before.

Q. *I am almost 60 years old and for health reasons have been forced to retire. I now feel lost, forlorn, of no value for anything or anyone anymore. I want to turn to God and dedicate the rest of my life to him. Is there some religious order that would accept me as a lay brother or oblate or something so that I could straighten out my life and prepare for death? I only have two children left at home. My wife is a teacher. We have a little savings so that I would not necessarily become a burden on some religious order.*

A.   What's your wife going to do while you bury yourself in a monastery? I am afraid you are the victim of the false notion that prevailed in the Church for so long a time, that only the religious can strive for perfection, that the only way to be holy and close to God is to flee the world. You will come closer to God by giving more of yourself to your wife, your children and your neighborhood, for that is your calling in life.

Volunteer your service to your church or some community project. There are lonely old people in nursing homes or maybe in your own neighborhood whom you can help with regular visits. Look around you and you'll find people who need you — if for nothing else than driving them to the store for groceries. Get involved in the lives of others and your own life will take on new meaning, and you will learn that the best way to prepare for death is to live life to the fullest.

Q. *I have the most wonderful wife in the world; we are both practicing Catholics and get along beautifully. But last year some friends talked us into attending a Catholic Pentecostal prayer meeting, which was attended by some 200 lay people, priests and nuns. They sang beautiful songs, read scripture and had a meditation period. Everything was fine until about 50 of them started to babble in "tongues." Then some of the people received a prophecy and said it aloud. My wife accepted this movement and decided to continue going. I had decided to go a few more times. Each time I went, I was turned off more and finally stopped going. I was hoping she never would get the "tongues" as I couldn't accept this. But she did. She doesn't babble at home but does at the meetings out loud with the rest. At home she babbles in her mind and also at work. She says speaking in tongues is a personal relationship with God that you get from no other praying. I couldn't believe this. This led to one argument after another. I told her I was going to pray to God to let her forget the "tongues" and be a normal practicing Catholic, and she said the Lord will never answer my prayers because this is a gift from him and he does not take away a gift.*

This is ruining our marriage. I found out a few weeks ago that the movement is causing dissension in other homes. Just what about this movement? And what do I do? I want to make my wife happy, but I know she won't be if I make her quit going.

A. The Catholic Pentecostal movement began in the United States in 1967. It spread rapidly. In 1969 the Committee on Doctrine of the National Conference of Catholic Bishops made a study of the movement and came to this conclusion:

"Perhaps our most prudent way to judge the validity of the claims of the Pentecostal movement is to observe the effects on those who participate in the prayer meetings. There are many indications that this participation leads to a better understanding of the role the Christian plays in the Church. Many have experienced progress in their spiritual life. They are attracted to the readings of the scriptures and a deeper understanding of their faith. They seem to grow in their attachment to certain established devotional patterns such as devotion to the Real Presence and the rosary. It is the conclusion of the Committee on Doctrine that the movement should at this point not be inhibited but allowed to develop. Certain cautions, however, must be expressed."

Your experience is probably an example of what the bishops had in mind when they called for caution. Speaking in tongues could be a gift of the Spirit, but it could also be merely an emotional reaction. Instead of arguing, you and your wife should sit down together and read chapters 12, 13 and 14 of Paul's First Letter to the Corinthians. These chapters were the inspiration for the Pentecostal movement. There one thing becomes clear: The purpose of the gifts of the Spirit is to promote love and unity. "If I speak with human tongues and angelic as well, but do not have love, I am a noisy gong, a clanging cymbal," Paul warns in 13:1. And St. Paul does not want a lot of babbling during the prayer service, which is evidently what was going on in Corinth. In

14:27-28 he writes: "If any are going to talk in tongues let it be at most two or three, each in turn, with another to interpret what they are saying. But if there is no one to interpret, there should be silence in the assembly, each one speaking only to himself and to God."

EQUALITY OF WOMEN

Q. *Please comment on this: "Wives must be submissive to your husbands; be subject to them as to the Lord . . ." The priest reads this at the wedding ceremony. This pagan concept in a Christian sacrament today is disgusting. Brides should refuse to countenance the reading of such degrading words. Even 2000 years ago this wasn't "truth."*

A. I think you will be pleased to know that a much wider selection of reading from scripture is now provided for the wedding Mass, so the passage regarding wives being subject to their husbands need no longer be used as part of the ceremony.

But you might also like to know how a passage like that got into the scriptures in the first place and what the force of such a statement is in terms of faith, since it seems contrary to the "true" notion of marriage, that is, the notion that is commonly accepted today.

In ancient times, rules for family and social relationships were set down in "household codes" which summarized the duties of a man as a member of human society. These codes provided standards of conduct for husbands and wives, parents and children, masters and slaves, and rulers and subjects.

Certain New Testament passages, including the one

you mentioned concerning husbands and wives (Eph 5:22), together with other statements dealing with women's clothes (I Tm 2:9), widows (I Tm 5:3-8), slaves and masters (I Tm 6:1 and I Pt 2:18-20), old people and young people (Ti 2:1-10), and civil authority (I Pt 2:13-17), contain precepts patterned after the common "household codes" of the time such as those of Epictetus and Seneca.

Since these codes appear in scripture as well as in secular writings, the question arises as to whether they are based upon revelation or whether they are simply customs and attitudes taken over from secular society and expressed in Christian terms.

The best opinion seems to be that Paul and the other writers who make use of these codes are not presenting this material as revealed truth but that they are rather urging Christians to experience the existing and accepted social structures of their time in a Christian way.

And so in their letters they attempted to provide a theological basis for the relationship of husbands and wives, parents and children, rulers and subjects which was taken for granted in first-century society.

Today, customs and attitudes have changed, and we must try to experience the social relationships of our time in a Christian fashion. Some of the new alternate readings for the wedding Mass bring this out quite well, I think, such as the passage from Genesis describing man and woman as being one body (Gn 2:15-24) or Paul's statement about the love of Christ being the source of hope (Rm 8:31-39) or John's remark's concerning the importance and beauty of human love (I Jn 4:7-13).

Q. *I have a problem in that I am both Christian and a woman. Christ himself treated women as persons, with a love and respect that gave them equality as human beings. Sex did not seem to be an issue. Then along came St. Paul with what I consider to be anti-women attitudes.*

Both Protestants and Catholics grant to every utterance of St. Paul an infallibility yet to be granted to anyone but a pope. Every priest, minister, bishop, pope, and active layman in Christendom swallows even the tiniest side opinion of St. Paul hook, line and sinker.

Well, I am a woman. I not only question the infallibility of St. Paul's words, but refuse to accept many of them. Last Sunday I was particularly irritated by the epistle which said that wives should obey and honor their husbands as the Church obeys and honors Christ. When he symbolically placed husbands on the level of God and wives at the level of a church made up of humans, I no longer wondered why the position of women in Christian cultures depends upon the whims of individuals and groups of men.

A. St. Paul was what no pope could be—with the possible exception of St. Peter, who may or may not be the author of the epistle attributed to him — the inspired writer of God's holy word. He was, therefore, as the whole Christian Church has always taught, not only free from error in his writings, but also was the means through which God revealed himself. You can't just write him off as someone whose thinking you don't like and remain a believing Christian.

But you are quite right, to my way of thinking, in resenting what the male-dominated Church has done with some of the teachings of St. Paul.

Like all the inspired writers of scripture, Paul was a man of his own times with all the limitations, prejudices and misinformation common to the culture and civilization of which he was a product. The Church has only recently grasped the significance of this, for in stressing that what the inspired writers of scripture asserted the Holy Spirit was asserting, men tended to think that everything the writers affirmed was necessarily inspired and free from error. This led to needless conflicts between religion and science, as those who accepted the bible as the authority not only on revelation but on everything from astronomy to hairdos, stood up against every advance in human knowledge.

The important constitution on revelation of Vatican Council II settled this problem for Catholics by teaching that "the books of scripture must be acknowledged as teaching firmly, faithfully and without error that truth which God wanted to put into the sacred writings for the sake of our salvation."

And to make clear what they meant, the Fathers appended as a footnote the following quotation from St. Thomas Aquinas: "Any knowledge which is profitable for salvation may be the object of prophetic inspiration. But things which cannot affect our salvation do not belong to inspiration."

It is hard to see how Paul's rule obliging women to wear hats in church and ordering them to keep silent had anything to do with the salvation of the human race. Much of Paul's thinking and many of his rules for the early Church merely reflected the common attitudes of his day.

It is not accurate, therefore, to argue from the pas-

sage where Paul forbids women to teach in church that
God has revealed to him they were not to teach and never
to be ordained. In the society in which St. Paul lived,
women were not to be heard in public and men were
supposed to have their hair cut short, etc. And he assumed that this is how things ought to be, just as doubtless he assumed the world to be a few thousand years
old and flat like a big saucer.

For this day what Paul had to say about marriage
was advanced and revolutionary. In the passage that
bothered you, St. Paul was not equating men with
Christ the God-Man; he was saying that men ought to
love their wives as Christ loves the Church. This was
making demands of men never made before. And by
comparing the union of man and wife with the union
between Christ and his Church, Paul gave a meaning to
marriage that added a dignity to women's role never
known before.

What is more, Paul is the one who insisted that
"there are no more distinctions between Jew and Greek,
slave and free, male and female, all of you are one in
Christ Jesus" (Gal 3:28). Now that I think of it, it seems
to me that St. Paul might even be a likely candidate for
patron of the women's liberation movement.

Q. *I have considered pursuing a form of Christianity
other than Catholicism. My frustration stems from the
fact that very little attention has or will be given to equal
rights for women in the Church. We have given much
to the Church for the past 2000 years and gotten little
in return. We cannot enter the sanctuary during Mass,
let alone serve as altar girls or even lectors in most
places. We are still treated as a separate "race," while*

in other sectors of society we are equal with men. When attention is given to us by the Church it is in the form of pedestal worshiping, which disregards the fact that we are human beings.

Therefore, I think I could be serving God better in a church that treats a woman equally, regardless of her sex, because in the eyes of God her soul is neither male nor female, and may I add that God himself has no sex.

A. Well, now, let's talk this over before you make a rash decision. It is true there is discrimination against women in the Catholic Church. The refusal to allow girls and women to serve Mass, the denial of the priesthood to women is really un-Christian, it seems to me. It is a cultural remnant from a pagan past, a part of our culture not yet leavened by the yeast of Christian ideas.

But Christianity is still in its primitive stage. We are the first Christians — if it can be admitted that the earth may go on supporting life for thousands or even millions of years. Women have already come a long way under Christian influence from the condition of inferiority they occupy in other civilizations. There are reputable historians who support the thesis that it was the devotion to Mary as the Mother of God, the exultation of a woman as the greatest of all Christians, that improved the lot of women in the Western world. Shouldn't you think twice before you leave the Church that seriously promotes that devotion?

You may find it possible to become a minister in some Protestant churches, but even here you will bump into discrimination and be forced to be satisfied with the position of minister of music or education, with far less prestige and influence than that enjoyed by a Catholic religious woman principal of a parochial school. I think we tend to overlook the opportunities afforded women in the religious orders. Where else can women have so many opportunities of becoming principals of schools, presidents of colleges, and administrators of hospitals? It is surely a curious and ironic twist of fortune that today, when they feel they must conform to modern ways to survive, the sisters are hiring male presidents for their colleges and male administrators for their hospitals.

Don't be hasty; don't sell the old Church short.

Q. *Some years ago there was a rumor that women were permitted to go to church without a covering on their head. Today about 90 per cent of the women are doing just that. According to Holy Scripture: "For a man to pray or prophesy with his head covered is a sign of disrespect to his head. For a woman, however, it is a sign of disrespect to her head if she prays or prophesies unveiled; she might as well have her hair shaved off. In fact, a woman who will not wear a veil ought to have her hair cut off. If a woman is ashamed to have her hair cut off or shaved, she ought to wear a veil" (I Cor 11:4-6). In the light of Holy Scripture, how do you explain that many women today worship in the Eucharistic community with heads uncovered?*

A.   It looks as though women are finally winning a battle they have waged a long time. The ladies of Corinth in St. Paul's time were forerunners of Women's Lib. The veil was the sign of the subordination of women to men. St. Paul heard that some of the Christian women of Corinth were imitating their local sisters who were defying male supremacy by appearing in public without veils. The fiery Apostle felt this was a serious threat to what he considered the divine order in which the female was subject to the male.

Like all the inspired writers of scripture, Paul was a man of his own times, with all the limitations, prejudices and misinformation common to the culture and civilization of which he was the product. In his world women were to be veiled as a sign of subjection, and Paul assumed that this is how things ought to be as he assumed the world to be a few thousand years old and flat like a big saucer.

In the past we Christians have presumed that the assumptions of the inspired authors of scripture and all that they taught were unchangeable and without error. But this is not so, as we are willing to admit today. Vatican Council II in the *Constitution on Revelation,* as noted in a previous question, teaches that "the books of scripture must be acknowledged as teaching firmly, faithfully and without error that truth which God wanted put into the sacred writings for the sake of our salvation." And to make clear what they meant, the Fathers of the Council, as also noted before, quoted St. Thomas Aquinas: "Any knowledge which is profitable for salvation may be the object of prophetic inspiration. But things which cannot affect our salvation do not belong to inspiration."

It was difficult to see how St. Paul's rule obliging women to wear veils in church to show their subjection to men has anything to do with the salvation of the human race. Especially is this so now that another teaching of St. Paul seems to have brought about a change in the status of women. His insistence that there is neither male nor female, neither Jew nor Gentile, but that we are all one in Christ, little by little after almost 20 centuries, has begun to have some effect on the thinking of Christians. In most countries where that thinking has penetrated, women no longer consider themselves subject to men, and the law requiring covered heads no longer has any relevance.

The law is still in the code of canon law, but church laws like civil laws cease to have effect when customs contrary to them are established. The women have concluded that the law on hats is about as relevant as laws regulating the tethering of horses in big cities.

Q. *Congratulations. I rejoice to see that there is one Roman Catholic priest who is courageous enough to state that the Church's myopic, misogynistic ideas about women could be wrong. For too long a lot of padres have quoted St. Paul's (in)famous words about silence and submission whenever Catholic women have dared to express their belief that their low status in the Church was the will of some men rather than part of God's plan. Take good care of yourself, Monsignor. With all the gynophobic Latin members of the hierarchy, we need you.*

A. I'm feeling fine, and so far no member of the hierarchy, Latin or otherwise, has complained.

Q. *A popular book on women's history quotes Gratian as follows: "Man, but not woman, is made in the image of God. It is plain from this that women should be subject to their husband and should be as slaves." Did the Catholic Church ever hold that women were inferior to men because they allegedly were not created "in the*

*image of God"? Please answer my questions. If you
do, I'll have something to show the anti-Catholic bigots
in my "lib" group. I am not a Catholic but I "stick up"
for the women who belong to your faith.*

A. The quotation is from a collection of ancient church
laws and customs put together around the first part of
the 12th century. It is a paraphrase of St. Paul's explanation of why women should cover their heads at worship.
In I Corinthians 11:7-10, he argues: "A man, on the
other hand, ought not to cover his head, because he is
the image of God and the reflection of his glory. Woman,
in turn, is the reflection of man's glory." Gratian gives
a twist to his interpretation, reflecting the pagan Roman
notion that wives were the subjects and property of their
husbands. His collection of laws was never recognized
as authentic by the Roman Church.

It must always be remembered that Christianity developed in a civilization that held women to be inferior
and subject to men. The Church, and no other institution, struggled against this notion and little by little
elevated woman's place in society. Your "lib" gals should
be told that it was the venerating of many women as
saints and the exaltation of Mary, the mother of Jesus,
by the Church which had much to do with the fact that
Western civilization arrived at a notion of equality between men and women. In a previous answer, I pointed
out the great contribution the religious orders of the
Church made to the advancement of women. In the
Middle Ages convents and monasteries were the centers
of formal education. There were more convents than
monasteries, and occasionally an abbess would be the
religious superior of men as well as women. The Church's

promotion of virginity, more than any other factor, surely advanced the recognition of woman's dignity and worth as woman rather than as wife.

Q. *Theologically speaking, which of the following statements is more correct: All mankind was created in the image of God or man was created in the image of God, woman was created in the image of Eve?*

A. Your first statement is correct: All mankind was created in the image of God. The first chapter of Genesis, which presents much more sophisticated and advanced knowledge of God and creation than Chapter 2, has this to say: "Then God said: 'Let us make man in our image, after our likeness. Let them have domination over the fish of the sea, the birds of the air . . .' God created man in his image; in the divine image he created him, male and female he created them" (vv. 26-27). Here man, male and female, "resembles God primarily because of the domination God gives him over the rest of creation," as the St. Joseph edition of the new American Bible notes.

The second chapter of Genesis, which is a much more ancient text and, therefore, more primitive, has the story of how Eve was formed from the sleeping Adam. The principal purpose of this story was to teach that women shared a humanity exactly like that of man, contrary to the contemporary belief of other nations that women were incomplete and inferior beings.

But in the course of time, when all the first five books of the bible were considered the writings of Moses, the Jewish people came to see in the second chapter of Genesis grounds for believing that women were the reflection of the glory of men. St. Paul expressed this thinking when he wrote in his First Letter to the Corinthians: "A man, on the other hand, ought not to cover his head, because he is the image of God and the reflection of his glory. Woman, in turn, is the reflection of man's glory."

Paul's words have had a most unfortunate influence upon the development of Christian thought regarding women. He was actually only trying to keep intact the traditions of the culture in which he lived and not expressing any revelation about how mankind is made to the image of God or what God has revealed about women. But it took the Church a long time to separate what was revealed in Christ from the culture and thought patterns in which the revelation was made. And this process is still going on. This is why I think the day will come when women will be ordained priests and bishops.

Q. *In his epistles, St. Paul repeatedly told slaves to obey their masters and women to be subservient to men. Why would an all-just, all-merciful God apparently authorize the oppression of slaves and women?*

A. You exaggerate. As far as I can find, St. Paul only twice advises women to be subject to their husbands and only once refers to slaves obeying their masters. But we won't quibble over this. Your problem arises from a misunderstanding of the inspiration of the bible.

God does not treat the inspired writers as puppets, but allows them to be true authors, who reflect the limited knowledge and ignorance of their times. As the Word of God, by becoming man in Jesus of Nazareth, limited himself and accepted our human weaknesses, so the Word put into human writing filters through the limited humanity of the inspired author.

As noted in previous questions, Vatican Council II teaches that "the books of Scripture must be acknowledged as teaching firmly, faithfully and without error that truth which God wanted put into the sacred writings for the sake of our salvation." And to make their meaning clear the Fathers of the Council appended a footnote from St. Thomas Aquinas as follows: "Any knowledge which is profitable to salvation may be the object of prophetic inspiration. But things which cannot affect our salvation do not belong to inspiration."

The human authors of scripture, like St. Paul, can fail to understand the full import of the inspiration they received and can be in error in matters that do not affect salvation. St. Paul lived in a world which accepted slavery and the subjection of women, as we in the Western world today accept capitalism and labor unions, as a part of life. He clearly taught that before God there is no distinction between male and female, slave and free but that all are one in Christ. However he did not see that this was inconsistent with slavery and subjection of women. It took almost 2000 years before this inconsistency became evident to Christians, and a lot of them have not seen it yet.

If you want to see St. Paul at his best regarding slavery read the much-neglected, short letter to Philemon. A slave of Philemon named Onesimus stole money from his master and ran away to Rome, where he was converted to Christianity by St. Paul. In the letter Paul tells his good friend Philemon he is sending Onesimus back and pleads that he forgive the slave and receive him no longer as a slave but as a brother. Paul does not com-

mand Philemon to do this, but he proves himself a master
of human psychology by the way he persuades his friend.
The precedent he set here surely had much to do with
the practice of the early Christians who did free their
own slaves and treated the Christian slaves of others as
brothers.

Q. *I read your discussion of St. Paul's teachings with
great interest. If more priests thought as you do, we
who seek to improve the status of women in the Church
would have no problem. Unfortunately, the reverend
gentlemen who possess the power to alter the rules
tend to oppose any measures opening the priesthood
to qualified women. To help reeducate our hierarchy,
several homemakers and I have founded an organization called T.I.G.R.E.S.S. (The Interdependent Gals Re-
jecting Evil Scholastic Sophistry). Together with our
husbands and children over 12, we have pledged to
give neither money nor any other form of support to the
Church until women receive equal rights and opportunities. In keeping with our promise, we shall send our
school-age youngsters to public institutions. Three
couples have revised their wills in such a way that their
bequests to Church-affiliated groups will be valid only
if women have been given access to the priesthood.*

A. Your observations are worth printing as a bit of
Church memorabilia. But if you value my opinion, I
hope you will pay attention to what I say. Your approach
to the problem of equality for women will cut you off
from all communication with the authorities in the
Church. I know enough about bishops and have read
enough about popes to assure you they will not be in-

timidated by your organization. You will become frustrated, embittered and eventually leave the Church, and then you will have no influence whatsoever.

You must work from the grass roots. Struggle to get women accepted as lectors and extraordinary ministers of the Eucharist. Urge your sisters to become members of parish councils. Clamor for the organization of a pastoral council for your diocese, on which women will be well represented as consultors to the bishop. All these steps are possible, for they are already permitted.

You live in a dreamworld. Most women themselves are unwilling to accept the idea of women as extraordinary ministers of the Eucharist. I say this with regret, but I face reality.

FAMILY LIFE

Q. *In view of the high divorce rate, wouldn't it be good for preachers to delete explanations of verses of the bible and pound home to husbands and fathers their responsibilities? We know a man who goes to Catholic church every Sunday, tries to imply he is religious and knows all about the faith, but we don't know of a wife and children who are more abused than his. He is so bullheaded; he's the only one who is ever right, never shows any love or affection, leaves for weeks at a time. His children are marrying outside the Catholic Church and giving up their religion; the families they marry into live by far better lives. Don't you feel as priests that you are remiss in not speaking more effectively? One priest said: "Make hell just a little hotter than it is."*

A. I don't think the temperature of hell will affect a

man like the one you describe. He is the product of parents who failed. His wife should see a priest and marriage counselor. For the sake of the children still at home, she may be advised to separate from him. The priest in the pulpit cannot do much for people like this man. All that the priest in the pulpit can do, it seems to me, is to help reduce the numbers of such people in the future by teaching that religion is meaningless unless it implies self-sacrifice and love of others and by urging parents to train their children in self-discipline and generosity.

Q. *I have a problem that is threatening to wreck my marriage. My husband, I and three small children live in a rural community that is almost 100 percent Catholic, and a Catholic fraternal organization is my problem, for it is encroaching more and more on the time that should be spent as a family.*

There are weekly card parties, monthly meetings, monthly stags, for which the wife must send meat and a covered dish along with her husband, and daily, except Sunday, opportunity to obtain legal beer and illegal mixed drinks. Each of the special events lasts until the wee hours of the morning, after which many cars are driven home with intoxicated men at the wheels.

I don't know how to fight this occasion of sin. The local priests support this type of recreation and the average Catholic considers a person to be half-baked if he doesn't actively support his local club.

A. Could you be exaggerating? If it's as bad as you paint it, the intoxicated drivers will soon kill themselves off, and your problem will be solved. Maybe your husband and a couple of cronies are staying out late and persuading you that all the other members are doing the same thing. You wives had better compare notes.

The source of your difficulty, however — and now I speak less prudently — is something deeper. Many of our Catholic fraternal organizations are floundering for lack of a purpose. They build expensive clubhouses for their own pleasure and amusement. Many of them no longer deserve tax exemption as charitable organizations. They should be building and financing centers for rural youth, organizing and backing centers in the inner cities, running homes for the rehabilitation of alcoholics, developing housing projects for the retired, if only for their own members, etc.

Q. *My husband passed away recently after many long years of suffering from a painful and incurable disease. Very few people except those close to him realized how terribly he did suffer. We knew he could not be cured, that his suffering would grow worse. He could find rest only in death. He talked to us about his condition, was resigned to it, and conscious almost to the last. He received the last rites and was well prepared to die.*

His family's problem now is this: We lived with him and suffered with him. No one will ever know how much. We accepted the situation as the will of God and for my husband's sake controlled our feelings during his illness and also at his death. We knew he would have wanted it that way. Now we are being criticized for our behavior.

We loved him and miss him terribly. But no one seems to understand how we can sit down and recall all the happy times we had together and talk about when we will meet him in heaven. We are happy his pain is

*over at last. Life or death has no fear for us because
he showed us how to live and die. Still the criticism
bothers me.*

A. It sounds to me as though you are surrounded by
a bunch of Gloomy Gus types who are secretly envious
of your serenity and strength. Try to ignore any critical
remarks and thank God you have such a deep understanding of what this old world's all about. Prolonged
illness and the death of a loved one are severe tests of
spiritual maturity. You passed both with flying colors.
There are not many who would do as well.

Q. *I am 28, have three healthy little boys, 4, 3, and 2.
I love them dearly and feel fortunate to have them. I
have been married eight years and my husband and I
have a wonderful and satisfying relationship. However,
at the end of some days, after screaming fights among
the boys, all the noise, work and worry, I am so nervous
I could scream and cry myself. Sometimes I even flip
out, holler at the boys, perhaps spank them unneces-
sarily and feel guilty after they are in bed. Am I normal
or do I need special help?*

A. Madam, you are perfectly normal. This is the
unanimous decision of six mothers in the same circumstances to whom I read your letter.

Q. *Our diocese plans to educate our children about
sex in our parochial schools from kindergarten on up
through high school. I have seen some of the slides
and materials that are being used in parochial schools
throughout the United States. Shocking is the only*

word I can think of to describe this literature. How the Catholic Church ever allowed this program into our schools is beyond me. We have opened our doors and exposed our children to filth.

When did God change the laws on chastity and purity? When did we parents give up our God-given right to teach our own children about sex and morality? Why were we not consulted on this program? Why is it such a big secret?

A. A long time ago, somebody got the idea that material things were evil. This strange belief began to spread, and we have been living with it in one form or another ever since. One of the most widespread expressions of this notion is that sex is nasty and that anything whatsoever that has to do with man's reproductive capacity is filthy.

Now this is odd, isn't it? When you consider that sexuality and reproduction are a normal, God-given part of the life experience of all living creatures, what can there be about these things that is nasty or filthy? It is hard to say, of course, unless there is something in the back of one's mind that tells him that they are closely connected with man's material body and, therefore, are evil. But so are eating, drinking, sleeping, and a number of other things.

A good sound program of sex education in the school can go a long way toward helping children grow up with a healthy idea of their sexuality. If they learn to regard sex as a normal and natural part of human existence and begin to understand its sacramental function in the context of married love, their lives will be much richer and, no doubt, holier for it. Sex is an essential part of our humanity. Our schools would not adequately educate our children to understand what it means to be human if they ignored something so essential.

Sex education is needed in the schools today precisely because too many parents have a jaundiced notion of sex. And those who have a healthier attitude are frequently too timid to deal with the subject and force their children to satisfy their natural curiosity in the alley or schoolyard.

The schools and school systems that I know of which have begun sex education programs have involved the parents every step of the way. The administrators realize that parents have the first responsibility for the education of their children. They are also aware that, in some cases, parents need to be educated as well as the children. I can't imagine why a school system would keep such a program secret and not invite the interest and participation of the parents. In a case like that, I might be inclined to be suspicious, not necessarily of the purpose of the study or the materials to be used, but rather of the attitudes of the administrators responsible for the secrecy.

I suspect, however, that you have been misled about the program in your diocese by some of the vicious, lying pamphlets circulated by the irresponsible groups that are campaigning against sex education in all the schools of the country under the ridiculous pretense that it is a communist plot to destroy the morals of the American people. In one of these you may have read that slides and materials used in parochial schools are shocking. Or one of the promoters of these may have shown you slides and materials purported to be used in parochial schools. If so, you have been truly misled.

There simply are no slides and materials being used in parochial schools throughout the U.S. It's hard enough to get the parochial schools in one diocese to follow a uniform program. No one would be foolish enough to try it for the whole country.

Be patient. I am sure you will be given an opportunity to see the materials used in your school.

Q. *My 10-year-old daughter is asking, "Why all the controversy over boys wearing long hair when pictures show Jesus wore long hair down to his shoulders?" Does anyone know this for sure? Was there a custom at the time of Christ for men to keep their hair long?*

A. Yes, and it was the custom for men to wear beards, too, at the time of Christ.

Q. *Does the Church still teach the Ten Commandments? My great-granddaughter came home from school and said there are not ten anymore, just two.*

A. The Ten Commandments still exist as part of the Old Testament teaching on man's duties toward God and his fellowmen. They are listed twice in the Old Testament in slightly different forms (Ex 20 and Deut 5) and are also mentioned in the New Testament, although they do not appear as a list of ten precepts as they do in the Old Testament.

For example, Jesus repeats the prohibitions of murder and adultery in his Sermon on the Mount (Mt 5:21 and 27); also Mt 19:18 and Mk 10:19 refer to five of the commandments.

Jesus said that he came not to destroy this Law but to fulfill it. When a man asked him how to be perfect, he said to keep the commandments. But Jesus also indicated that something more was demanded of his followers than mere slavish obedience to the letter of the Law. Those who obey all of the commandments and do no more are like slaves who simply do their basic duties (Lk 17: 7-10).

Jesus' friends will look beyond the letter to the spirit of the Law and will be willing to go farther than, say, the Scribes and Pharisees who emphasized the observance of all the small points of the Law while seeming to miss its essentials. These essentials, which Jesus said summarize all the Law and the Prophets, are love of God and neighbor, the two great commandments. This is what your great-granddaughter undoubtedly referred to. Read the account in Mt 22:34-40.

While some of the Ten Commandments deal with love of neighbor, Jesus taught that this includes even one's enemies (Mt 5:43-48; Lk 6:27ff; Lk 10:29-37) and, in saying this, he was adding a new dimension to the Law as stated in the Old Testament.

So you cannot say that Jesus abolished the Ten Commandments. Christian tradition continued to accept the decalogue as a basic code of morality. However, Jesus made it clear that he expects more than mere legalistic observance from his followers, and this "more" is indicated by his explanation of the great commandment of love.

Q. *I am very much against the trend in our parochial schools to eliminate the obligation of daily Mass for the children. The school Mass in our parish has been elim-*

*inated and the children are encouraged to attend
weekday Mass voluntarily.*

*Well, the children are obliged to wash behind the
ears, brush their teeth and keep regular hours for meals.
Is this going to harm them? We grown-ups are obliged
to keep traffic laws, be at work on time, etc. Does this
harm us?*

A.   Without realizing it, you have put your finger on the
reason why pastors and religious educators are experi-
menting with voluntary daily Mass for their school
children. They don't want children to equate Mass attendance with the routine of brushing teeth and obeying
rules. Are your children obliged to kiss you at certain
times of the day or week? Are you training them to
show you affection? Weekday Mass, some think, is this
sort of thing. It is something the children should do out
of love, not routine.

Who knows whether this new approach is best? One
thing we do know is that teenagers no longer take the
Sunday Mass obligation as seriously as we oldsters did
when we were their age. We had better find ways, therefore, to help children of today *want* to attend Mass.

Q. *We have a little girl who is two, a baby of seven
months and now expect another child. Of course, this
is too many too soon and my husband and I realize it
more than anyone else. However, we try to be cheerful,
do the best we can and put ourselves in God's hands.*

*Everyone in the family is very upset. My mother and
father especially and also his mother. Our strong moral
support comes from two dear friends, a man and wife*

with two children. These people are Protestants and, believe it or not, we have received more encouragement and strength from them at this time than from those so near and dear to us. Would the Church permit at least one of these good people to act as the new baby's god-parent? There is nobody I would rather have "stand" for this new babe than one of these dear friends.

A. Yes. So long as there is one Catholic to act as an official sponsor, our Church now permits a Protestant to serve as a "Christian witness" at a baptism. I don't see why both could not serve as witnesses along with the sponsor. You have a mighty good reason for wanting Protestants for this baptism. And I hope your parents read this and find out why.

Q. *How can I reconcile the fact that so many of my faith—Catholic—are selfish and un-Godlike toward me and my family due to our unfortunate situation of hav-ing a disabled husband and father to my children?*

My family though well off has not been able to cope with this fact and refuses to do anything to aid in our dire need. Yet my mother attends Mass and the sacra-ments regularly with a feeling that she is in perfect har-mony with everything around her. To me they have be-come despicable people. What would it take to make them see this plight?

A. Maybe they will see this appeal for help and recog-nize their neglect. Your letter reminds me of the Corin-thians who would not share their food with the hungry in the "love meal" that preceded the Eucharist in the first days of the Church. St. Paul (1 Cor 11:27) puts it to them bluntly: "Whoever, therefore, eats the bread or drinks the cup of the Lord in an unworthy manner will be guilty of profaning the body and blood of the Lord."

If your relatives are actually ignoring your need, then they fall under Paul's condemnation every time they approach the altar and they had better heed the advice of the Lord: "So, if you are offering your gift at the altar, and there remember that your brother has something against you, leave your gift there before the altar and go; first be reconciled to your brother, and then come and offer your gift" (Mt 5:23-34).

Q. *Have you found the postconciliar changes threatening the solidarity of family life? I refer particularly to a situation where a spouse rejects almost totally the updated Church, while the other partner accepts all or some of the present-day Catholic viewpoints. Would not the religious attitudes of the children be based on uncertainty in a case such as this?*

A. The children growing up in such a home may be better prepared to live in the Church of the future than those in homes where both parents are in complete agreement, either for or against the changes.

The Church of the future will be a Church of unity, we hope, but not of uniformity. The trend today is to encourage diversity and variety in worship, devotions and forms of penance. The elimination of the Lenten fast and the Friday abstinence in favor of personally chosen forms of self-denial is an example of what I mean.

Provided the parents who differ in their attitudes about the changing Church can live together in peace and respect for one another's opinions, where better than in the home you describe can children learn how to avoid the polarization that threatens the Church today?

Yes, the postconciliar changes can threaten the solidarity of family life, but they need not.

Q. *Billy Graham answered someone who wanted to know how we can love and fear God at the same time by saying: "Fear and love are reverse sides of the same coin and there should be no conflict." And he said: "If a child doesn't have a bit of awe and respect for his father and mother, it is doubtful if he loves them as he ought." And I seem to remember the scriptures saying: "The fear of God is the beginning of wisdom." But our new Catholic religion books for little children no longer teach the fear of God. As one priest said: "They don't teach little kids to fear God. They teach them that God the Father loves them, that he is their friend and protector." What are we doing to our little ones?*

A. Before an infant learns to have awe and respect for his parents he first of all discovers that his parents love him, feed him, protect him. As his intelligence grows he develops the sense of awe and respect for those upon whom he depends.

The same process would seem best for learning about God. The little child must first learn that God loves him and supports him. Then as he grows and his intelligence develops he must be taught that the response to this love is respect and awe and fear of displeasing so great a lover. And that's what the new religion textbooks do for the older children. A six- or seven-year-old is not ready for wisdom; when he is comes the time to teach him fear of the Lord.

To introduce a little one to God by immediately teaching him to fear him might have much the same disastrous results as trying to teach parental respect by spanking a week-old baby. A child must have trust and love for his parents before he can ever learn the proper fear that leads to respect and obedience. Without this trust and love the fear the child has leads to disrespect, disobedience and sometimes even hate. There are too many bitter adults today who turned from God and religion because they were taught to fear him before they learned to love and trust him.

Q. *When I was young I was told that if I lied or did something wrong, God would punish me. If I fell down, it was God who pushed me, etc. Every accident meant I had done something wrong in his eyes.*

A. Incredible. You were misinformed. Parents or teachers who make God out to be a policeman are refusing to do their own job. They should train children in the basic, natural virtues of honesty, truthfulness, reliability, punctuality, etc., the same way and with the same means they teach them to brush their teeth, wash behind their ears and observe good manners.

When they are older and have learned these basic habits, through the seat of their pants if necessary, they can be shown how what they have learned helps them love others and thereby love God. In my opinion to use God as a policeman to train youngsters in the basic moral virtues is to corrupt both religion and morals.

Q. *I come from a family where unfortunately my father works almost all the time. My mother in his absence has over the years become a dominant person. I have*

*only one sister and a brother who have moved away
so that dominance has affected me greatly.*

*I'm 18 years old and since the sixth grade I've had
problems with sex identity. For seven years without
anyone knowing, I dressed up in my sister's clothes. I
didn't really know I had a problem and I didn't know
why, but I've grown older and closer to God. With his
help I am conquering this problem by not doing it anymore. I would only wish that parents who read the
letters you get could understand their children better,
mothers to let fathers live their lives as "Dads" and not
forget that you were the one that said "yes" when he
asked you to marry him.*

A. In the hope that young mothers will be helped to
avoid the mistake your mother made, I am happy to
share your letter. Over-domineering mothers can cause
a number of abnormalities in their children.

Q. *I wish to comment on the advice you gave a young
man whose problem was sex identity. He apparently
blames his domineering mother for his problem, and
evidently you agree with him. May I remind both of you
gentlemen that the mother probably became domineering because the father refused to accept his share of
the responsibility. The young man stated that his father
works "almost all the time." I doubt that the situation
is that desperate.*

*Too many fathers today feel their responsibility to
their families ends with the paycheck. Unfortunately my
own husband falls into this category; and my children,
while considerably younger than your letter writer, have
recognized this fact. Before placing all the blame on*

*the domineering mother, remember the doormat father
must bear equal responsibility. In order to become a
doormat one must first lie down voluntarily!*

A. My ears are burning. I'll be more careful in the
future. I really wasn't condoning the father; I was trying to help mothers like you — and unfortunately there
are far too many — by warning them of the danger they
face when they are obliged to make up for a missing
father.

Q. *Please say what a family should do when the father
comes home drunk and abuses three sons, 12, 15 and
17 years old. If he wants to strike the mother is it wrong
for the oldest son to push him back or punch him away?
This boy is about to enter college and does not smoke,
drink or take drugs. I do not believe that the alcoholics
do not remember the next day. Furthermore, how often
can you forgive in 20 years? I am an interested friend.*

A. A son should, if he is able, defend his mother from
the abuses of a drunken father. No woman should ever
have to put up with beatings from her husband, drunk
or sober. Frequently the only answer to a problem like
this is a restraining order against the husband and an
appeal to the courts for a legal separation or perhaps
even a divorce. The woman should discuss her problem
with her parish priest. I have read articles by reformed
alcoholics who claim they do blank out and cannot remember the next day what they said or did while under
the influence.

Q. *I know of a young couple who have tried in two dif-*

ferent churches to have their young son baptized. The wife who is not a Catholic was married before, but her marriage was annulled in the courts. The husband is a Catholic, but because of her previous marriage could not be married in the Church. But why deny baptism to his son? Here are two young people trying to do what is best for their son, and we shut the door. Must an innocent child be the victim? I always thought we never refused to make everyone a Christian.

A. Priests are not permitted to baptize children indiscriminately; they must have some assurance that those who present children for baptism will bring them up in the faith. It would be interesting to know all the circumstances in this case. Maybe the Catholic father wants the son baptized but the mother is determined to bring him up in some other Christian Church. I must admit, however, that I have known of pastors who would not baptize the children of invalid marriages. How they can make a rule of this I don't know. They are wrong and were badly taught.

I suggest you talk with your friends and if they are determined to bring the boy up in the Catholic faith help them find another priest. Surely, all the priests in your locality were not taught by the same mistaken professor of church law.

Q. *I am a non-Catholic married to a Catholic. However, I attend the Episcopal church every Sunday. Your answer to the parents who wanted their child baptized but were not married in the Catholic Church is just one of the reasons I am not a Catholic. In the first place, baptism is not for the parents' benefit, but for the child's. Whatever the parents' reason, who is the priest to judge which child should be baptized and which should not?*

If you and other priests like the one who refused to baptize this child would think more of Christ's rules and less of the Church's rules and rights to regulate people's lives, you would antagonize fewer people and bring more people closer to the Church.

A. I have discussed your letter with Episcopal priests and Protestant ministers. They agree with me that baptism is too important to be given to infants without some discussion with the parents about their intentions of rearing the child a Christian. Baptism is, indeed, for the benefit of the child; it makes the child a member of the Church. This will not benefit the child, however, unless he has a chance to learn what the Church is and what membership in it entails. Unless the parents have some interest in the Church, therefore, it would seem far better to let the child grow up and seek baptism for himself.

This suggestion, I know, creates problems for those who believe that infants who die without baptism cannot enter heaven. But today more and more the opinion prevails that a merciful God has his own way of saving these innocents. Our Church, taking no chances when salvation is at stake, still requires that infants be baptized as soon as possible and immediately in case of danger of death, and yet at the same time forbids the baptism of infants without the consent of the parents.

Parents have a mighty important part to play in the baptism of an infant in our new Catholic baptismal rite. They must make a profession of faith in the principal beliefs of the Church; they must promise to bring the child up in the faith they profess. Unless their profession of faith is sincere, it would be a mockery; unless their promise is serious they would be acting a lie. So for the sake of the parents wanting a baby baptized it would seem that the Christian thing for a priest to do is to make sure they know what baptism of infants means. I am convinced that it will be rare that the priest cannot help the parents seek baptism with the right dispositions or recognize honestly that it would be better to wait awhile.

Q. *Can anyone deny a child a sacrament if his parents do not attend so-called preparation meetings for the sacrament? We, like many other parents in our parish, feel these meetings are ridiculous and a waste of time and do not intend to attend them and be treated like children. Why should a string be attached to a sacrament, when as a baptized Catholic a child has every right to go to confession, receive First Holy Communion and the sacrament of Confirmation?*

A. As parents you have the right to obtain the sacraments for your children, but you also have the obligation to see to it that the children are properly prepared for the reception of Holy Communion, Penance and Confirmation. Your parish priests have the obligation to see to it that you are able to prepare your children properly. That is why they arrange classes for parents and expect them to attend.

You are not being treated as children; you are being given an opportunity to bring your own knowledge of the sacraments up-to-date and learn how to use to best advantage the books your children will study from. School teachers, as you know, are required to attend workshops and lectures to learn the newest techniques of teaching and how to use new textbooks. You as teachers of religion to your children ought to welcome the opportunity your priests are offering you.

Your attitude shows that you have much to learn about your religion. The sacraments do not work like magic. To receive them fruitfully a person must have a knowledgeable faith and an intelligent response. Help yourselves and your children to benefit more from the sacraments by enlarging your knowledge of the faith.

Q. *You dodged a question. Can the sacraments be denied children because their parents do not attend meetings helping them prepare children for Baptism, Penance, Communion and Confirmation? In our parish these sacraments are denied. How about it, yes or no?*

A. To be consistent with my answer to the previous question, I must state that parents have the first obligation and, therefore, the first right to decide whether their children are ready for the sacraments. The pastor has a right to question a child if he has doubts about whether it is prepared, but I believe he is denying the rights of parents and children if he refuses the sacraments solely on the grounds that the parents have not attended a preparation class.

Notice I said solely on the grounds that the parents did not attend the class. Refusal to attend the class might very well indicate the parents are not sufficiently interested in the faith to be serious about the promises they must make in the case of Baptism to bring the child up in the faith. In such a case, a pastor should refuse. But should this matter be decided on who has rights and obligations? Are we not all interested in the spiritual welfare of the children? Today, with new rites for the sacraments and fresh understanding of how they work, few parents are ready to prepare their children without help. The very ones who think they are, most likely are not aware of the changes and hold tenaciously to the notion that the sacraments work like magic. In conclusion, I should like to point out that the inspiration for the preparatory classes comes from Rome. The Sacred Congregation for Divine Worship in its instruction for the new rite of baptism of children states that it is the duty of parish priests "with the assistance of catechists or other qualified lay people, to prepare the parents and godparents of children with appropriate pastoral guidance . . ."

Q. *As I read your answer to the parents about preparation for Holy Communion, I was puzzled. Why is the preparation for Communion shoved off onto the parents? So the nuns have more time to gallivant around?*

A. According to the old law of the Church, which prevailed even when nuns wore habits, the parents and confessor are to decide when a child is ready to receive Communion. A pastor has the right to question the child if he has doubts about its readiness. But note that the parents must first make the decision to present the child. The new rite for baptism of children stresses the obligation that parents accept, by presenting their children for baptism, to train them in the practice of the faith. The parents, not the parochial schools, have the obligation to teach the faith to their children. Sisters and other religious teachers are helping parents fulfill this duty.

Q. *What is the teaching of the Church about a baby who dies without baptism? When I was a child we were taught such a baby would go to Limbo.*

A. Neither scripture nor the oldest Christian tradition directly deals with the question of what happens to unbaptized children, though both stress that salvation comes from Christ through union with the Church that one enters by baptism. St. Augustine reluctantly taught that these infants are condemned to a part of hell where pain would be minimal. This doctrine in the course of centuries was mitigated by those who held that unbaptized children would live on in a place of their own, called Limbo, where they would not see God face to face but would enjoy a natural happiness.

Today the existence of Limbo is questioned by many distinguished theologians, who base their opinion upon the revelation that God wants all men to be saved and that the human race as a whole was redeemed by Jesus Christ. Now that the Church quite generally holds that adults who know nothing of the need of baptism are saved through the baptism of desire, these theologians suggest the possibility of a special baptism of desire for infants who may obtain the use of reason at the moment of death or, in the case of infants of Christians, the desire of the parents that their child be saved. The official teaching Church has so far not favored the new opinion but allows inquiry to continue among theologians. It must, however, be admitted that with the new rite of infant baptism, which places so much emphasis upon the willingness of the parents to raise the child in the faith and the practice of refusing baptism for infants whose parents are not serious in their intention to raise them as Christians, the trend now seems to favor the conviction that God in his own way will take care of infants who die without baptism.

Quite frankly, we must admit we are dealing here with a question that has not yet been settled. To be safe we baptize dying infants even without the parents' request and yet we assure Christian parents whose infant died without baptism that a merciful God must have his own way of giving eternal life to the little one.

Q. *In your recent comment on what the Church's thinking today may be concerning the future life of infants who die without baptism, you overlooked the texts for funerals of children who die before baptism in the new Rite of Funerals.*

A. Thanks to an illustrious canon lawyer and liturgist. What I find is truly encouraging for the parents of such children. Among the suggested readings are these words of Isaiah 25: "On this mountain the Lord of hosts . . . will destroy the veil that veils all peoples, the web that is woven over all nations; he will destroy death forever." (The Gospel suggested recounts how the veil in the temple was torn in two from top to bottom.) And this from the Book of Lamentations 3: "But I will call this to mind, as my reason to have hope: The favors of the Lord are not exhausted, his mercies are not spent." And this suggested prayer: "Father of all consolation, from whom nothing is hidden, you know the faith of these parents who mourn the death of their child. May they find comfort in knowing that you have taken him (her) into your loving care."

It is most significant that the new Rite of Funerals includes a Christian burial service for unbaptized infants. Not only was this missing in the old rite, but church law did not allow Christian burial for such infants. This change is a good example of how the speculation and study of theologians eventually bring about changes in the thinking and practice of the official Church.

Q. *We have six married children who attended Catholic schools for 12 years. Three of them are divorced and remarried. Now one of the children not divorced tells us parents who are in our 60's that we should not be friends with the divorced members of the family, that we should not accept them in any way and that if we do we are not any better than they are. We say it is not Christian to act this way and do not want to be separated from any of our children. There is a lot of friction going on among our children and some of the grandchildren are deeply hurt because they want to see their aunts, uncles and cousins. What does one gain by not caring for the lost sheep?*

A. You have solved your own problem, which is what persons in your situation must do for themselves. You must love the children who have made mistakes and want to help them to stay as close to God as they can in their unfortunate situation. Once you have made clear to them that you regret that they have done what they did, you should remain close to them so that you can encourage them to raise their children in the faith. It seems to me that if you cut yourself off from the divorced members of the family, as the one child advises, you will lose all influence for good over them and embitter them against the religion that inspires such action.

PARENTS AND THEIR TEENAGERS

Q. *At what age does a parent drop the last responsibility to an offspring? When am I obligated to "leave them be" as the song says? At present, I am all shook up from my children's refusing to listen to calm, good guidance. Our oldest is 17 and is constantly leaving me with the impression that I am to "leave him be." I realize that many young people are of the same nature. I am beginning to doubt my own good judgment due to his ways of helping others before he helps members of his own family or even tries to strengthen his very own ethics and morals.*

A. So long as they are minors and have not established a home for themselves, you have a responsibility to direct and educate your children as best you can. But, it would take a Solomon to answer your question adequately.

Most teenagers want some direction and discipline, such as hours to come home by — though they rarely admit it. But they also need to experiment, to take chances, to discover for themselves what life is all about. And here is where the tension with parents arises. Some parents are oversolicitous; they worry excessively about the harm that might come from the mistakes their young will make. They become too strict and demanding; far from trusting them, they give the clear impression they are sure the youngsters are going to do wrong. This is perhaps the worst mistake parents can make, worse than being too trusting and lenient. The young want to be trusted; they must be trusted if they are ever to mature.

I suggest you praise your 17-year-old for the good things he does for others; don't be jealous, show an interest in what he does. The morals he learns at this age are going to come more from your example than your commands.

All this, I know, is easier to say than to put into practice. We do what we can with teenagers, and leaving the rest to God we trust that, as in the past, most of them will miraculously turn into sensible men and women.

Q. *Please help me find peace of mind. I lost my husband many years ago; he was not of my religion. My two sons gave up the Catholic religion. One is dead. The other is married to a non-Catholic. What can I do? Will God ever forgive me? I go to Mass and Communion every day, but find no peace. I feel that I am the cause of all this and am so frightened as I am near 80 years old.*

A. You must trust in the goodness and mercy of God who forgives you whatever mistakes you have made in the raising of your sons and who surely can find a way to save them. You should not blame yourself too much. You had a difficult task rearing two boys in the Church without the help of a father. Keep on attending Mass and receiving Communion as long as you can, praying each time for your sons, living and dead.

Q. *The man who is dating my daughter is married and the father of two children. He does not live with his wife but at home with his parents. I confronted my daughter and it seems to make little difference to her. I also spoke with the gentleman but got nowhere. They no longer attend Mass and spend a good deal of time together as they both attend the same Catholic college. This man no longer calls for her at our home. How do I handle this situation looking at it from a Catholic view? I cannot be a hypocrite and accept him into our home.*

A.   Other than pray, there is very little that you can do. You have made your mind clear to your daughter. Any opposition from now on, more than likely would strengthen her determination to stay with this man. You are right in closing the door to him.

Q.   *Our daughter, aged 13, is extremely fascinated by the "Jesus Movement." She volunteered to be on the debating panel at school in favor of this movement. A teenage group of her friends has invited her to the meetings, which are held every night, and she has been told they consist of about a 45-minute prayer, after which there are discussions and just "sitting around and talking," but no drugs, etc. She is pressuring us into letting her attend one of these meetings to get material for her debate and, as she says, she just wants to see what it is like and what other people do. Would it be all right for us to let her go to one of these meetings, or is it wrong in any way?*

A.   You are the only ones who can make such a decision, for you know your daughter and how mature and well grounded in her faith she is. We should be grateful there is a Jesus movement, for it is helping some of the young to discover that Christ has a meaning for them today.

Perhaps we need to apply to ourselves in this case the advice Jesus himself gave the Apostles when they had problems about a similar difficulty: "John said to him, 'Teacher, we saw a man using your name to expel demons and we tried to stop him because he is not of our company.' Jesus said in reply: 'Do not try to stop him. No man who performs a miracle using my name can at the same time speak ill of me. Anyone who is not against us is with us' " (Mk 9:38-40).

Q. *What are your views of seminarians (college age) dating girls and girls dating seminarians? We are parents of both.*

A. I am against it until the day arrives when celibacy becomes optional for the Catholic clergy. I know that the seminarians today who do date argue that they need the experience for their own proper maturity. But there is a partial answer to this now available from the sociological study of priestly life made for the National Conference of Catholic Bishops.

This study, which reports that "the majority of the priests do not accept the present position on obligatory celibacy and expect that a change in the law is likely," has this to say about our problem:

"There is no evidence in our research that Catholic priests are deficient in emotional maturity when compared with other groups in American society.

"No evidence could be found that either early entry into the seminary or dating experience affected either emotional maturation or personal morale among the clergy."

I believe that the almost total isolation of seminarians

from women as it used to be was a mistake (though obviously not a very harmful one, if the bishops' study is accurate). And I approve the trend today to give college seminarians an opportunity to experience a more normal education with regular college students, both men and women.

Q. *If you were a parent and had children of college age, would you send them to Catholic universities to be taught by "order" priests and progressive nuns, who would encourage them to question, to probe, to use their own intellects and their own consciences, or would you send them to secular universities and to Catholic student centers or Newman clubs run by diocesan priests, where they would graduate geared to the parish-level mentality, docile and happy to obey the voice of the Church? There is just about a thousand dollars a year difference between the two methods.*

More and more parents who have sent young people to Catholic colleges find them coming home full of questions and speaking a language different from that of older Catholics. The Newman Club members seem happy to take the word of the priest as law. Is this good?

A. A college education is supposed to prepare young people to take their place in the modern world and, hopefully, to make some kind of contribution to that world. The kind of education you seem to prefer would prepare the young to live in the past rather than in the present.

There was a day, not long ago, when a kind of naive docility was considered virtuous for a Catholic. He was supposed to pay, pray and obey and leave the thinking to someone else. Vatican Council II recognized that those days were gone forever. In *The Constitution of the Church* the bishops teach that today's Catholic is expected to be a thoughtful, responsible, mature participant in the affairs of the Church. And rightly so. Rote answers and a closed mind can do little to promote the cause of Christ in a world that demands reasonableness and initiative.

Priests and sisters in college work, or any other teachers for that matter, who do not encourage young people to question and to probe and to make use of the new biblical knowledge and the advances in theology to understand their faith would be preparing them to practice religion in a world that no longer exists.

If I had the responsibility of selecting a college for a young person today, I would not make my choice on the basis of "order" priests or diocesan priests but rather on the kind of education offered by various colleges. My choice would be for the college which best prepared its students to live as mature Catholics and productive citizens in today's world.

Q. *How can I help our son nearly 19 return to assisting at Sunday Mass and the sacraments? He has been neglecting his religious duties for months. Everything I try to encourage him in fails. He simply refuses. He is a good boy and had religious training. I pray daily for him to return to his faith.*

A. You have lots of company, for many other parents are facing the same problem. The young have always expressed their need for independence by refusing to observe the rules of their elders. Missing Sunday Mass was one way Catholic youths asserted themselves. The revolt of youth today against the establishment is stronger than any of us oldsters remember. It should not be surprising, therefore, that more young people today than ever before are staying away from Mass. For them the Church is part of the establishment.

You won't accomplish anything by hounding the boy. Let him alone. He'll return to Mass on his own or he'll never return. Persuade him with your example. As he grows older and discovers that you are wiser parents than he thinks you are now, he may want to return to the religion that helped make his home the pleasant place he remembers. The best thing you can do for him now is to show him that your own faith helps you create a pleasant home. Sociological studies have shown that most people who give up the religion of their childhood come from unhappy homes.

Q. *Why is it our children of today say they get nothing out of going to Mass? They go elsewhere to try to find themselves. I think the priests are to blame when they get to the pulpit. They hurriedly read what's in the bulletin and announce a second collection, and that's it. It's sad when they are so educated in theology and share so little of their knowledge with their parishioners.*

A. Surely there must be some priests in your part of the world earning their keep! Priests are obliged to see to it that a sermon is preached at the Masses on Sunday and are encouraged to give a short homily even at weekday Masses. Shop around a bit. A pastor who does not himself or arrange for others to preach each Sunday deserves to have an empty church.

Poor sermons or the absence of sermons may drive some young people from the Church, but I fear you are oversimplifying the problem. There are many reasons why the young are not interested in the Church. Some feel the Church has failed to live up to their expectations; some are in revolt against the Church because they are in revolt against their parents or against society as they find it. All reasons why we priests must speak to the problems of the day.

Q. *What do you do with a 16-year-old girl who won't go to Mass anymore?*

A. Demonstrate to her by the way you live that going to Mass makes you a more loving, generous parent and neighbor. Be serious about this. Ask yourself how you act on Sunday after Mass, and what Sunday is like in your house, and what effect Sunday Mass has on the rest of your week.

Call her attention to youth Masses when scheduled. Invite her to go with you occasionally. But don't argue with her. Don't threaten or nag. Don't try to force her. Pray for her instead.

RETARDED CHILD

Q. *I came down with German measles while pregnant and went to a priest for advice. When he told me it would be a mortal sin to have an abortion even to avoid bringing a deformed child into the world, I followed his advice. So we have a severely handicapped child. You can imagine how I and a thousand like me must feel when you tell the woman who had an abortion years ago she may now go to confession. You say: "Go and sin no more." It would have been far better for us and our child if we, too, had the abortion. We didn't sin; we had our child. Others sinned, but now you give them absolution. Explain that to our handicapped child.*

A. I'd like to begin my answer by sharing with you the response I received from the woman who was afraid to confess the sin of her youth and had given up hope. This is what she wrote: "You were right about everything. The confessor was happy he was the instrument through which I was reconciled with God. I am filled with joy and can hardly wait for each morning to awaken and live my faith."

It strikes me that we have here a modern version of the Parable of the Prodigal Son. Remember what happened when the wayward son returned and his father welcomed him with a big banquet. The faithful elder son complained bitterly to the father: "For years now I have slaved for you. I never disobeyed one of your orders, yet you never gave me so much as a kid goat to celebrate with my friends. Then when this son of yours returns after having gone through your property with loose women, you kill the fatted calf for him." "My son," replied the father, "you are with me always and everything I have is yours. But we had to celebrate and rejoice. This brother of yours was dead and has come back to life. He was lost and is found" (Lk 15:29-32).

This parable shows how penetrating is the insight of Jesus into human character; he understands your feelings. But it also reveals the mysterious love of God. "My ways are not your ways" God kept trying to convince the Chosen People through the whole history of salvation. The life, death and resurrection of Jesus is a demonstration of what God is like and how he loves. His love is quite other than ours. We love because we are attracted by the goodness and lovableness in other persons. God does not love us because he finds anything lovable (in us or because we have done something that makes him love us. He loves us because he is what he is. And because he loves us we become lovable. "In loving me, you made me lovable" was the way St. Augustine expressed it in his *Confessions*.

I like to think that parents, or those who take care of a deformed or retarded child are given the opportunity of loving more as God does than the rest of us. For by loving the child they succeed in making the deformed person lovable — as many of them, indeed, really are. So count your blessings as well as your burdens. You have the satisfaction of knowing you did what you felt was right no matter what the risk. And now you have the opportunity, with the help of God which must be offered you in abundance because you were generous, to understand better than most mortals of how God loves.

I can't explain that to your handicapped child. You by your love are the only ones who can make life meaningful for him. And if you continue to make an effort to do that, then surely you will want to rejoice with sinners who are transformed by God's love.

Q. *After reading your advice to the mother of the handicapped child, I feel compelled to reply to the mother involved. I, too, was smitten with German measles in the first trimester of my seventh pregnancy.*

Our little Jude arrived early in 1959, with the possibility of being microcephalic. By the end of the first year, the sword did pierce, and our fears were realized.

An amazed intern, viewing a family snapshot, stated, "But you could have had an abortion legally." Murder — and that's what it would have been — never entered our minds. And I'm wondering, outside of God, who can determine for sure that a fetus will be deformed.

In the passing years our family cared for our little one and gave him love. And he in turn responded, seemingly understanding our love; in fact, taught us the art. We laughed when he laughed, were saddened when he cried, and heartsick when he was ill. Time lapsed, and soon we were seeing the inevitable handwriting on the wall. We were being forced to face the facts. Jude was preparing for his final journey, and once again we felt the pierce of that sword. How we would miss doing for him, holding him, pressing him close, kissing him, fondling the soft curls — and in the last weeks, drying the solitary tear that would appear.

On Sunday, November 25, 1973, on the Feast of Christ the King, God called him home. Jude, too, had to die to really begin to live. And through our tears we were truly happy for him, rejoicing in his victory. Here lies the solution to the entire situation. Jude's death certificate read in part: "Cerebral Palsy and profound mental retardation." You see, what the body appears to be means very little to God. It's the beauty of the soul that counts. We should not be concerned with the few short years the body (deformed or perfect) has on earth but for the soul, destined for eternity.

So, grieved mother of that deformed child, take heart. If he is capable of understanding, assure him of

*your love for him and of God's love for him in sending
this cross for him to carry. When death comes to claim
your youngster, only then will your little one realize
the value of his existence, and he will be eternally
grateful.*

A.   Amen.

Q. *I read with interest your reply to the women who
had a deformed child as a result of German measles,
but I feel that one aspect of why there are handicapped
people was missing from your article. While God permits sin and evil, I have come to think that he not only
permits but also wills that handicapped people be a
part of today's society. Handicapped people have a
special ability to share in the sufferings of Christ and
help others to grow in a better awareness that this
life on earth is not the ultimate and end of all things.
So, in themselves the handicapped people can, in St.
Paul's words, "fill up what is wanting in the sufferings of
Christ."*

*The handicapped person needs much help in his
physical life. By accepting this help, the handicapped
is God's instrument in accepting the kindnesses of
those willing to help: "Whatever you do to the least of
these little ones, you do unto me." Even those who are
unable to respond to God's love in full understanding,
such as the mentally retarded, can be the object of
love — love that can be given not only to them but also
to God who lives in these simple souls.*

*In answering the woman who does not know what
to tell a severely handicapped child, it may be helpful*

to her to explain as best the child can understand that God permits him to be born in this way as a special sign of God's love for the child and wanting the child to share in his cross in a special way. While accepting the needs that must be rendered him, the child should be taught to learn that he, in return, should accept such help gratefully, while remembering in prayer his helpers. In this way there is an even balance, as the able-bodied help the physically handicapped in his daily life, and in return the handicapped helps his benefactors through his prayers and cheerful acceptance of all that God asks of him.

The handicapped person has much to contribute to today's society and spirituality if more stress is placed on his obligations rather than on his disabilities. I write this as a person who has been physically handicapped from birth and as a member of The Catholic Union Of the Sick In America, Inc. CUSA is only one of many apostolates which embody both the spiritual and social aspects of the life of a handicapped person.

A. Those interested in The Catholic Union of the Sick in America may write to 184 E. 76th Street, New York, N.Y. 10021.

part 4
Birth Control

Birth Control

BIRTH CONTROL

Q. *Recently in conversation with a group of friends I mentioned that according to the bible the first man who practiced birth control was struck dead by the Lord. I quoted: "He withdrew and threw his seed to the ground and was immediately struck dead." No one in the group had ever heard of such an instance. Is there such a text in the bible?*

Q. *Genesis 38:8-10: "Then Judah said to Onan, 'Go to your brother's wife, perform your duty as brother-in-law, and raise up descendants for your brother.' Onan knew that the descendants would not be his own, so whenever he had relations with his brother's wife, he wasted his seed upon the ground, in order not to raise up descendants for his brother. What he did was evil in the sight of the Lord, and he killed him also." Why does not the Holy Father's* Humanae Vitae *make mention of this verse from the Holy Bible which gives the pronouncement of Almighty God himself on birth control as*

158

a basis for the Church's and hence the Pope's teaching?

A. It is not at all certain that Onan was punished for spilling the seed. Scripture scholars today are all but unanimous in holding that Onan was struck dead for refusing to raise up a son for his brother. According to an ancient law that the Jews followed, when brothers lived together and one of them died without a son, another brother was obliged to marry the widow and the first son born would succeed to the name and inheritance of the dead brother (Deut 25:5). Onan's sin was the refusal to fulfill this law.

It is significant that Pope Paul did not refer to any scripture passage in his encyclical *Humanae Vitae.* There does not seem to be anything in scripture clearly referring to the problem of birth control. The Pope based his argument upon "natural law" known through reason.

Q. *Recently I was told that a couple marrying in the Church were validly married even if at the time of marriage they had every intention of using contraceptives. How can this be? Aren't they violating a law on marriage?*

Would one be bound in conscience to report this to the pastor before the marriage should he know that a couple intended to use contraceptives? Could a pastor refuse to have them married? I am invited to such a wedding.

A. An intention to exclude perpetually the right to have children would, according to our church law, invalidate a marriage. If a couple planned to use contraceptives so long as the woman could bear children with the intention of never having any children, they would not enter into a valid marriage. It is not the intention to use contraceptives, but the intention to exclude children that would invalidate it.

You probably have in mind the use of contraceptives throughout married life to limit the number of children. A couple doing this would be violating a law on marriage, but would not invalidate the marriage.

There would be no obligation to report this to the pastor. A pastor should instruct such a couple concerning their obligations, but he has no right to refuse to let them marry in the Church. The man and woman have a God-given right to marry; they do not lose this right even though they may intend to abuse it.

There is a possibility that the couple feel they are justified in planning to use contraceptives. You should not judge them. And this you might be doing if you stayed away from their wedding.

Q. *My husband has had a drinking problem for six years. Every weekend is spent in the local bar and sometimes several nights during the week. We practiced the rhythm method until it failed. A brother and sister marriage will not work. After my last two pregnancies I had nervous disorders caused by hormone upsets. Each took about a year to cure, with heavy expense. This condition can recur with another pregnancy. My older children wish me to receive Communion with them. If I do so, do I commit a sacrilege?*

A. It is obvious that you want to abide by the teaching of the Church. It is possible to respect this teaching and still decide that to avoid greater evils you must put up with the evil of artificial birth control.

Pope Paul in his encyclical *Humanae Vitae,* gave the moral principles concerning birth control in the light of which Catholics should form their consciences, but he did not discuss the question of the good faith of those who make practical decisions in conscience against what the Church considers the divine law.

Following the encyclical the various national bishops' conferences issued directives to help couples apply the teaching to individual circumstances. For example, the French bishops declared:

"Contraception can never be a good. It is always a disorder, but this disorder is not always culpable. It happens, indeed, that spouses see themselves confronted with veritable conflicts of duties . . . On this subject we shall simply recall the constant teaching of morality, when one has an alternative choice of duties, and whatever may be the decision, evil cannot be avoided, traditional wisdom makes provision for seeking before God which duty in the circumstances is the greater. Husband and wife will decide at the end of a common reflection carried on with all the care that the greatness of their conjugal vocation requires. They can never forget or despise any of the duties in conflict. They will therefore keep their hearts disposed to the call of God, attentive to any new possibility that might lead to a revision of their choice or their behavior."

Canadian bishops said this to their people: "In accord with the accepted principles of moral theology, if these persons have tried sincerely but without success to pursue a line of conduct in keeping with the given directives, they may be safely assured that whoever honestly chooses that course which seems right to him does so in good conscience."

As I said in a previous discussion of this problem several years ago: "You will note that in all this teaching, man does not make up his own morality and decide for himself what is right or wrong. He experiences a crisis precisely because he wants to follow the papal teaching on birth control and yet at the same time fulfill what he knows to be moral obligations to preserve his marriage and raise his children properly. Here is where even one who accepts the direction and teaching of the Church must still make decisions for himself."

You can make such a decision. Your reasons and circumstances certainly seem to be serious enough to feel in your heart, as you say, that you should be able to receive Communion. In other words, you have decided that you are not acting morally wrong. Abide by your decision.

Q. *I've always thought two children were a perfect little family. Is it a sin to limit your family by the rhythm method?*

A. How many children you should have is something that you and your husband with the help of God must decide for yourselves. Some couples need to plan their families more than others. Any number of Catholics today have decided in good faith that the threat of overpopulation requires them to have smaller families than their parents had. Others, frightened by the alarming drop in the birth rate and the increasing selfishness of young married couples, think they must be generous and make up for the many who refuse to have even the so-called ideal of two children. Vatican Council II offers this advice:

"They will thoughtfully take into account both their own welfare and that of their children, those already born and those which may be foreseen. For this accounting they will reckon with both the material and the spiritual conditions of the times as well as of their state in life. Finally, they will consult the interests of the family group, of temporal society, and of the Church herself.

"The parents themselves should ultimately make this judgment, in the sight of God. But in their manner of acting, spouses should be aware that they cannot proceed arbitrarily. They must always be governed according to a conscience dutifully conformed to the divine law itself, and should be submissive toward the Church's teaching office, which authentically interprets that law in the light of the gospel."

The Church, as you know, does accept as moral the rhythm method of family planning.

THE PILL

Q. *What is the Church's stand on the use of oral contraceptive pills as a therapeutic measure when severe menstrual irregularities make the practice of rhythm very unreliable?*

A. Physicians prescribe the use of what you call contraceptive pills for several therapeutic reasons. You may safely follow such a prescription even though the pills have a contraceptive effect. What you intend directly is the cure of the disorder. Moral theologians of recognized ability (and therefore experts whose opinions may safely be followed) teach that the "pills" may be taken to regulate the menstrual cycle as an aid to the use of rhythm.

Q. *I want you to comment on the following question and answer that appeared in our local secular paper.*
"Q. I have been told that the Vatican is financially interested in pharmaceutical houses which manufacture the birth control pills condemned by the Pope. Can you check this one out? T.L.L., Los Angeles, Calif."
"A. The Vatican has a financial interest in the Institute Farmacologico Serono which manufactures the pill. The president of the institute is Prince Giulio Pacelli, nephew of Pope Pius XII."
Could you verify the accuracy of this matter? If the answer is affirmative how can we as Catholics justify the apparent hypocrisy in this case?

A. I have no reason to doubt the accuracy of the answer; it is the question that is inaccurate. The Pope did not condemn "the pill." He did not mention the pill in his encyclical, *Humanae Vitae.* What he condemned was the use of anything other than abstention for contraceptive purposes.

The pill has other uses than contraceptive. It can be used to aid conception; in fact, it was originally designed for that purpose. It is frequently prescribed by doctors to relieve menstrual distress and other female disorders. It may be used to regularize the menstrual cycle and thus make the rhythm method of spacing births possible for couples otherwise unable to use it.

If the pharmaceutical house headed by Pacelli was reaping a profit from the pill because many bought it for contraceptive instead of therapeutic purposes, then you must admit that the Pope made his decision on birth control without any thought to financial considerations.

Q. *I want to go to confession, but I have a problem. I am convinced I am not sinning by using a birth control pill. But a priest told me I cannot use the sacrament of Penance until I stop using the pill.*

A. If you were convinced you were not sinning by using the pill, why did you confess it? I suspect you have some doubts. Talk your problem over with some other priest, who may be able to help you decide one way or another what you must do. If you are sincerely convinced that you are doing the right thing by using the pill, then you have no sin to confess. Go to confession, if you wish, and confess what you know to be sins.

Q. *Now that I have entered into the period of my life called menopause, the "rhythm" method no longer is practical for me and my husband. We have three very nice and much grown-up children and feel it would be an injustice to a child should we have one at this stage of our lives. The only help we got from our doctor was "your chances of becoming pregnant are so minimal"— which doesn't help at all after the fact. So what do people do at our ages? We would very much appreciate knowing the right thing to do.*

A. I presented your problem to two respected gynecologists who are trusted by Catholic patients. They both say that the anovulant pill is indicated as a helpful medicine for many women during the menopause. If your doctor advises this, you have an answer to your problem, for you need have no moral qualms about using the pills for this purpose.

These drugs are synthetic counterparts of natural hormones and may be legitimately used in the treatment of various menstrual disorders. If sterility follows from this it is not directly intended. One might also argue that nature does not intend a woman to conceive during the menopause, and therefore that the pills could be used to assure that nature functions properly.

Q. *I am a person with inner conflicts. Ever since I was a little girl my nerves have troubled me. I need direction and advice on my current conflict. I married a Catholic at the tender age of 16 and became a convert. I think I achieved some inner peace till the time came that I had five children. I had to choose between separate bedrooms and the pill. I opted for the pill. That was five years ago. Since then we have not been to church and our five children have had no religious training. I felt there would be no more family religious spirit as I couldn't receive Holy Communion with them.*

A. Your letter reminds me of a cartoon that appeared after Pope Paul issued his encyclical, *Humanae Vitae,* repeating the Church's condemnation of artificial birth control. It showed a stern-faced Paul VI wagging a finger, with a caption reading: "The pill is a no-no."

That rather crudely expresses the popular notion of the Catholic Church's teaching on birth control. It is a distortion, an oversimplification; it is unfair to the Pope; and it has done untold harm to persons like yourself who because of it have made decisions which have warped their own or their family's lives or to those who have ignored the Church's teaching on family life, if they have not turned the Church off entirely as a teacher of morality.

Far from forbidding Holy Communion to couples who may find the papal teaching more than they can bear, the Holy Father wrote: "Let them draw from the sources of grace and charity in the Eucharist. And if sin should still keep its hold over them, let them not be discouraged, but rather have recourse with humble perseverance to the mercy of God, which is poured forth in the sacrament of Penance."

And the advice he had for priests is most important. Urging them to proclaim the Church's teaching without watering it down, Pope Paul added: "But this must ever be accompanied by patience and goodness, such as the Lord himself gave example of in dealing with men." And he pleaded: "In their difficulties, may married couples always find, in the words and in the heart of a priest, the echo of the voice and the love of the Redeemer."

This, it seems to me, should put an end to the practice, followed by some priests, of advising persons with your problem to stay away from the sacraments until they change their minds.

Since Pope Paul's encyclical represents the present official teaching of the Church, it is important that we know precisely what aspect of morality *Humanae Vitae* is dealing with. The English moral theologian, Father Kevin Kelly, in a recent issue of *The Clergy Review,* writes: "The encyclical is not concerned primarily with subjective morality (i.e., whether this action is a personal sin separating this man or woman from the love of God) but with objective morality (i.e., whether this way of acting fully respects human values)." Theologians all teach that it is possible to perform an objectively evil act without sinning subjectively when circumstances and conditions influence the person acting.

Father Kelly notes that a comparison with the teaching of Pope Pius XI in the encyclical *Casti Connubii* is most revealing. The 1930 encyclical taught: "that any use of matrimony whatsoever in the exercise of which the act is deprived, by human interference, of its natural power to procreate life, is an offense against the law of God and of nature, and that those who commit it are guilty of a grave sin." Pius XI made an immediate transition from "objectively evil" to "subjectively sinful." Pope Paul avoided this. He makes no mention of sin with reference to the married couple except in the context of God's mercy when, in the passage quoted above, he encourages those who find it difficult to live up to the ideal of married life to frequent the sacraments.

He seems deliberately to have left to other teachers in the Church the pastoral problem of how to help individuals apply the teaching of the Church to their own unique circumstances and problems. And the bishops of the world responded with guidelines on how to interpret the encyclical. Though some episcopal conferences were clearer than others, they all agreed the individual conscience still had responsibilities in regard to applying this law as with any other law.

In a previous answer to a similar question I quoted the French bishops as follows: "Contraception can never be a good. It is always a disorder, but this disorder is not always culpable. It happens, indeed, that spouses see themselves confronted with veritable conflicts of duties. . . . On this subject we shall simply recall the constant teaching of morality, when one has an alternative choice of duties and whatever may be the decision, evil cannot be avoided, traditional wisdom makes provision for seeking before God which duty in the circumstances is the greater. Husband and wife will decide at the end of a common reflection carried on with all the care that the greatness of their conjugal vocation requires. They can never forget or despise any of the duties in conflict. They will therefore keep their heart disposed to the call of God, attentive to any new possibility that might lead to a revision of their choice or their behavior."

The Canadian Bishops put it this way: "In accord with the accepted principles of moral theology, if these persons have tried sincerely but without success to pursue a line of conduct in keeping with the given directives, they may be safely assured that whoever honestly chooses that course which seems right to him does so in good conscience."

Just recently Archbishop Michael Gonzi of Malta issued an instruction for the Maltese stating that if in their enlightened conscience "the married couple conclude that in their case the more urgent duty and the greater moral value which they must safeguard are the unity and stability between them and their family and that they recognize with penitence and humility that in their particular situation it is impossible for them to realize completely the ideal of married life as expounded by the pope's encyclical, they will not be guilty of sin and as such they should not consider themselves unworthy of receiving Holy Communion."

The bishops are not trying to undermine the teaching of the Pope; they are working with him as fellow bishops completing the work he began. Father Kelly quotes the French Jesuit, G. Martelet, whom some commentators regard as one of the inspirers of *Humanae Vitae,* as saying that many directives on the encyclical by the bishops of the world are a marvelous demonstration of collegiality in the Church.

It is a pity that the responses of the various episcopal conferences of the world have not been made easily available to married people. You are a Canadian. Had you read what your own bishops said you would have been able to avoid the mistake you made.

STERILIZATION

Q. *An appeal was made through this column to "some bright theologian" to solve the problem of a woman with three children whose non-Catholic husband wants to have himself sterilized to avoid a further pregnancy of his wife.*

Here is some practical advice for the wife:

1. Sit down and think about how lucky you are to have three lovely children.

2. You are not committing any sin if your husband, over your reasonable protests, has himself sterilized or uses contraceptives. As his wife it is your duty to stay with him in accordance with your solemn marriage vows and for the sake of your children. You may even have marital relations while he is using contraceptives, so long as you have let him know that this is against your religion and so long as you try to persuade him in a friendly manner that he should not use the contraceptives. Even more so if he has himself sterilized over your protests it is still your duty to be a devoted wife

*as before, and you should under no circumstances feel
bitter about this or make recriminations for the rest of
your married life.*

*3. If your husband is honestly convinced that, in
accordance with his religion, he is not doing wrong by
having himself sterilized to avoid any more children,
then he, too, does not commit any sin.*

A. A knowledgeable gentleman from California was
responsible for that answer. I find myself in complete
agreement with his advice and more than ever convinced
that today's educated layman must be consulted in matters of faith and morals. The appeal to "some bright
theologian" elicited a multitude and a great variety of
responses. Here are some samples:

"No theologian can be honest and tell this woman
what she wants to hear. She has a decision to make for
which she alone is responsible, and she alone will bear
the long-range effects. When a woman finds herself in
such a desperate situation, it is only natural that she will
turn to a magic cure-all, the pill. Today's women find it
much easier to put their faith in objects, such as the pill,
rather than in Jesus Christ where it belongs. . . . I am not
a celibate theologian, I am a happily married mother of
four children. . . . The years may bring a deeper understanding of our sexuality that will render the present
contraceptive craze to be looked upon as inhuman, yet
comic and certainly in many instances tragic."

* * *

"What is needed instead of a theologian is a literary
genius who can inspire the teachers of the Church to
admit a mistake has been made and to present a more

realistic position in such a manner as to let the Church save face."

*   *   *

"Most people take it for granted the worst thing that can happen to a person is to have too many children. I was one of those people at one time. I seriously considered having my husband do what your husband wants to do. By God's grace I changed my mind. . . . We had a lot of troubles and ten children. I am 36 years old now; my baby is 11 months old, and my husband has developed a consideration and love for me that has finally brought him over to my way of thinking, while God has finally developed a faith and trust in me that can take me through a lot of things that we have to go through in this world."

*   *   *

"Many prominent theologians, members of the laity and members of the hierarchy have indicated the need for revision of the Church's stated position on birth control. But the Church is the people; the Church is not simply a few hierarchs in Rome. So the consensus must be known."

*   *   *

"I too remember the days and nights when I would be almost sick with worry over much the same thing. I would talk to my pastor and he would offer no solution and very little sympathy. I finally decided that if I was to find the answer it would have to be directly through God. . . . Well, I did find my answer through my own conscience, and I think I am a better wife, mother and perhaps even a better Catholic because of it. I am not sure this lady will find the same answer that I did, but please tell her if she will put herself and her family into God's hands she will find peace of mind."

Q. *I have a problem and have not the courage to ask anyone in the know about it. My husband had a vasectomy a year ago. It does not affect him, for he never received the sacraments anyway. I always did. He goes to church for the sake of the children, but with neither of us now receiving Communion the older children no longer go. I feel if I could go back to receiving the sacraments the children would too. But can I? I realize my sin is as great as his because I gave my full consent to the operation. At the time it seemed to be the only answer.*

A. There is nothing you can do now to rectify the situation except to be sorry for your sin. Get to confession and return to the sacraments. Marriage relations are not forbidden to you now even though you were responsible for your husband's sterility. Make amends by the love and care you give to the children you have.

Q. *My husband would like to have a sterilizing operation. He needs my signature. I hesitate to do this for fear of excommunicating ourselves from the Church. We have a family of five children. Is there any way we could receive permission from the Church? Would we be excommunicated?*

A. No one in the Church can give permission for this operation. You would not be excommunicated for cooperating in this action, but you would be doing something the Catholic Church officially still considers immoral. Whether it would be sinful in your case is another question.

Father Bernard Haering, certainly a respected theologian, teaches in his book, *Medical Ethics,* that there are times when sterilization seems to be the best answer to a moral dilemma. When the "direct preoccupation is responsible care for the total health of persons or for saving a marriage (which also affects the total health of all persons involved) sterilization can then receive its justification from valid medical reasons." "If, therefore," he adds, "a competent physician can determine, in full agreement with his patient, that in this particular situation a new pregnancy must be excluded now and forever because it would be thoroughly irresponsible, and if from a medical point of view sterilization is the best possible solution, it cannot be against the principles of medical ethics, nor is it against 'natural law.'" He even recommends that "when his wife's health or other grave reasons make it clear that to risk any more pregnancies would be irresponsible," the man submit to a vasectomy since it is the simpler operation. Other leading moral theologians are now teaching that when there seems to be no other solution, a married couple could decide that a sterilization would be morally justified. Whether I agree with this opinion or not, I am obliged to tell you about it because it is a good probable opinion which you could use to help make a decision.

Q. *Can a woman who has had her tubes tied, which prevents pregnancy, still receive Communion worthily? If the answer is yes, then why can't any woman have this done, confess it and go to Communion again?*

A. Any sin can be forgiven if one is truly sorry for what one has done — even having one's tubes tied. There might be some question about how genuine the sorrow was to one who deliberately and coldly planned what she knew to be an immoral operation with the intention of going to confession immediately after and taking up a religious life as before.

Nevertheless, if after doing what was evil, she recognized with the help of God that she had acted immorally, sincerely regretted what she had done and sought God's forgiveness, she could worthily receive the sacraments again.

Q. *I think you were very unfair in your answer to the question about a woman having her tubes tied. Although I had no thoughts of this when I had my eighth baby at 38 years of age, and even though we were very happy with our other children, ages 6 to 18, and our new little girl, I did not want any more children. Because of this and a problem of varicose veins and leg ulcers the doctor suggested the tubal tie and thought I should have it. My husband and I decided to have it done. It never entered my head that it was "evil," as you put it. I still don't think it's "evil." I did not go to confession about it because I don't see anything to confess, and I still go to Communion.*

A. Since you did not know that what you did was considered morally evil by the Church and, indeed, thought that what you did was the right thing to do, you did not commit any sin. You have nothing to confess now. Keep on receiving Communion.

I did not want to be unfair to the woman who asked

about the morality of tying the tubes. The Catholic Church officially teaches that direct sterilization is immoral. The Holy Office declared in 1940 that any direct sterilization, whether of a man or woman, whether perpetual or temporary, is forbidden by the law of nature. Pius XII reaffirmed this in 1951 in an address to a convention of midwives. Up till now this teaching has not been changed. It may be changed someday, for it is not an infallible teaching. But until it is changed, Catholics are obliged to give serious attention to this teaching in making a moral decision about submitting to sterilization.

Indirect sterilization is permitted. This is a sterilization that is not directly intended but follows as a result of a surgical removal of a diseased organ, such as womb or tubes.

Q. *Your decision about the sinfulness of having a tubal ligation was of special interest to me. What about a deliberate but not cold decision after much soul-searching to have this done?*

I feel I have not sinned. I have not felt the need to confess in order to go to Communion regularly. I have three small children and can afford financially and spiritually no more. Is heaven lost to me?

A. Of course not. As I said before, God will forgive any sin that we are sorry for having committed. In your case there does not seem to be any sin to be sorry for.

If you honestly came to the conclusion that what you did was the right thing to do, then you acted correctly according to your own conscience. If you knew that the Catholic Church officially teaches that direct sterilization is immoral, I trust you took this into consideration when you made your decision. It is not an infallible teaching, but it is the official stand of the Church at this time, and, therefore, a Catholic cannot remain faithful if he refuses to pay any attention to it.

You may have found yourself in such a bind that you decided the only way you could fulfill other moral obligations you judged more important was by submitting to the operation. Even though I and others might disagree with your decision, you had to follow the judgment of your conscience.

Many would disagree with your action on grounds other than the moral teaching of the Church. There is something so permanent about what you have done. What of the future? What if you should lose the children you have through an unfortunate accident? Since there are other means of limiting the size of a family, I am sure there are many who would at least question the wisdom of what you have done.

Q. *In a pamphlet advocating eugenic sterilization I read the following: "Primitive and pagan peoples castrated boys to produce eunuchs. Roman Catholics continued the practice until modern times to provide male soprano voices for their cathedral choirs." Could this possibly be true and, if so, why does the Church condemn sterilization today?*

Q. *I would like to know for how many years the Vatican had the Sistine choirboys castrated. What was the Church's excuse for such an immoral practice that ruined the lives of so many boys who could never marry and live normal lives?*

A. Who's stirring up all this trouble? These are but two of six similar questions coming from six different sections of the country.

It is true that the Sistine choir in Rome and other church choirs in Europe, especially from the 16th to the 18th centuries, used castrated males for soprano parts. The "castrati" were highly paid and much in demand for opera and choral work. Moral theologians of the times wrestled with the moral problem this created. The majority of them declared the practice seriously evil, though a few, such as the Jesuit Thomas Tamburini, justified it on the grounds that the Church tolerated it by using these singers in church choirs.

The official Church did not recommend that young men be castrated, but we must honestly say that it did tolerate the practice. So we must admit, with John J. Noonan in his book *Contraception,* that in Christian Europe for several centuries "there was a tolerated belief that for purely economic advantage, a man might permanently incapacitate himself from procreating."

This was a mistake, as we see it today, just as the Church's toleration of slavery for so many centuries we now consider a mistake. For someone who looks upon the Church as a pilgrim, as St. Augustine described her, pressing on to an ever better understanding of who Christ is and what it means to be a Christian, it is consoling to know that the Church advances in the knowledge of what is right.

ARTIFICIAL INSEMINATION

Q. *I would like to know what the Church's position is regarding artificial insemination.*

A. Pope Pius XII flatly condemned artificial insemination when the donor was not the husband. In the case of artificial insemination with the husband's sperm, he was vague: "One does not necessarily proscribe the use of certain artificial methods intended simply either to facilitate or to enable the natural act effected in a normal manner to attain its end."

Father Bernard Haering, one of the leading Catholic moral theologians, has this comment to make in his recently published *Medical Ethics:* "It seems that Pope Pius XII wanted, above all, to exclude a voluntary ejaculation as a means of obtaining the sperm to be used for artificial insemination. But since then, within Catholic circles, a new approach has been found relative to voluntary ejaculation, which is still the clinically indicated method for obtaining sperm for fertility tests and for diagnostic purposes."

Here I must point out that the recent code of ethics for Catholic hospitals endorsed by the United States Bishops forbids this clinical method. However, enough of the highly respected Catholic moral theologians of the world are teaching that voluntary ejaculation is not morally wrong when its purpose is to promote fertility to create what is known in theology as a probable opinion that may be safely followed to make a moral judgment. So, a Catholic couple or Catholic doctors could act upon this opinion in places where the Catholic hospital code does not apply.

Father Haering is expressing the thinking of many sound theologians when he writes in the book referred to: "There are no convincing arguments to prove either the immorality of ejaculation by the husband in view of fatherhood or the immorality of introducing that sperm into his wife's uterus. It cannot be denied that our feelings, so deeply conditioned by tradition, rebel when faced with such an unusual problematic. However, we have to see the loftiness of the parental vocation as an essential part of marriage, and the immense joy of the husband and wife who, for years, have desired children and through this manipulation are now able to receive their own child in an atmosphere of genuine love."

part 5

Abortion

Abortion

ABORTION

Q. *In discussion concerning abortion, some Catholics have admitted that there might be doubt about precisely when a fetus becomes a human person. Does not the Church's definition of the Immaculate Conception of the Blessed Virgin settle this for us? The Church teaches that from the moment of her conception the Virgin was free from sin. Isn't this saying that from the moment of her conception she was a human person since only a person can be freed from sin?*

A. Duns Scotus, the great Franciscan theologian, was the staunchest advocate of the doctrine of the Immaculate Conception. Unless I am greatly mistaken, he was among the scholastic theologians who held that the human fetus was not animated by a human soul until it was completely formed.

The Church in defining the doctrine of the Immaculate Conception did not intend to determine the moment when the human soul is created. Her belief about the Virgin is that at the moment she did first come to exist as a human being she was filled with grace. You are taking the word conception to mean the moment when the female cell is fertilized. The Church in her definition does not use the word in such a restricted sense but rather as referring to the whole process of gestation.

Q. *Is it true, as Senator Robert Packwood of Oregon said on the Dick Cavett Show, that the Catholic Church did not come out against abortions until 1860 and before that permitted them up to 40 days for a female child and 80 days for a male child? On another TV interview show some "expert" claimed that St. Thomas Aquinas advocated and approved abortion.*

A. The Church has consistently from the beginning declared abortion immoral but it has not always attached canonical penalties to the offense.

There was unanimity among the Fathers of the Church (the bishops and scholars whose writings reflect the early belief of the Church) that abortion is immoral, but there was some dispute whether it is murder. They made a distinction between a formed and unformed fetus. The formed fetus was said to be ensouled and therefore human. To kill it was considered murder. And to this crime were attached certain canonical penalties. A local Spanish council at Elvira (about 300), for example, imposed a penalty for abortion of excommunication until death.

The distinction between formed and unformed fetuses seems to go back to Aristotle, who taught that the soul informed the male 40 days after conception, the female

after 90 days. This was changed by the Church to 40
and 80, in keeping with the purification customs of the
Jews.

Until the end of the 16th century, canonical
penalties for abortion varied considerably and were not
universal in the Church because of the lack of certitude
regarding the time of ensoulment. But this did not mean
that abortion was not judged immoral, for it was uni-
versally condemned. Pope Sixtus V (1585-90) imposed
severe penalties on any form of abortion. This pope was
a bit of a tyrant, though a well-intentioned reformer.
Some of his severe penalties against abortion were relaxed by subsequent popes, but the excommunication
against abortion remained. Pope Pius IX in 1869 re-
tained this penalty against the procurers of abortion when
he revised the list of excommunications.

St. Thomas Aquinas was among those Christian
writers who did not consider all abortions murder. Following Aristotle, he held that the fetus went through
stages in the process of becoming human. In the first
stage the fetus was animated by a vegetable soul, then by
an animal soul, and finally when sufficiently developed,
by a human soul. Hence, Thomas did not look upon an
abortion in the earlier stages as homicide. But he clearly
condemned abortion at any stage as immoral and against
the life-giving process.

Having said all this I must, in all honesty, tell you
that the Church did through the years permit what was
called indirect abortion. "Indirect abortion" was rather
widely interpreted until the end of the 19th century.
From the 14th century many Catholic theologians allowed both embryotomy (mutilation of the fetus) and

abortion to save the mother's life. This was interpreted as indirect abortion, for it was considered similar to killing someone threatening your life to preserve your own. In this case you were not considered directly killing another human being but directly intending the saving of your own life. The great moral theologian, St. Alphonsus, considered abortion to save a mother's life as indirect abortion, since what was intended was the saving of the life of the mother. This was considered common and free opinion in the Catholic Church until almost the end of the 19th century. Rome gave express approval to this opinion until 1872. It was not until 1895 that the Holy See condemned the theological opinion permitting therapeutic abortion to save a mother's life. I am relying for this information upon *Human Life* by John F. Dedek, published by Sheed and Ward, 1972.

Q. *What is the Church's teaching on the existence and status of the soul of an aborted child? Should it be baptized?*

A. No one knows at what moment in its development the fetus is fully human with a soul that is immortal. But the Church takes no chances; she directs us to baptize an aborted fetus, at least conditionally, saying: "If you are alive" or "If you are human, I baptize you . . ."

Q. *Are there any specific references to abortion in the Old Testament? I've been told of a reference in Exodus, but can find only chapter 21, verse 22, referring to men fighting and a pregnant woman being injured.*

A. You have found the only reference to miscarriage in either the Old Testament or the New, and, as you discovered, it does not refer to abortion. "When men have a fight," the passage reads, "and hurt a pregnant woman, so that she suffers a miscarriage, but no further injury, the guilty one shall be fined as much as the woman's husband demands of him."

The first teaching against abortion in Christian literature appeared about the year 100 in the *Didache,* where it was clearly stated: "You shall not slay the child by abortion. You shall not kill what is generated."

Q. *In an answer some time ago you wrote: "No one knows at what moment in its development the fetus is fully human with a soul that is immortal." But the definition of the dogma of the Immaculate Conception reads: ". . . the Blessed Virgin Mary, in the very first moment of her conception . . . was preserved immune from all stain of original sin. . . ." It would seem to me that we must conclude, therefore, that the Blessed Virgin Mary was a human being with an immortal soul from the very first moment of her conception. Otherwise the definition of the dogma would be something like: ". . . the Blessed Virgin Mary, in the very first moment of her ensoulment . . ." Isn't it true that the dogma implicitly declares that all persons are human beings with an immortal soul "in the very first moment of conception"?*

A. If you are identifying conception with the moment of fertilization, the answer is, no. Pope Pius IX was not attempting to decide the biological problem about when conception takes place, but defining that the Blessed Virgin from the first moment of her existence as a human being was free from original sin.

The great theological discussions that took place during the Middle Ages over the Immaculate Conception were between theologians who for the most part did not think that hominization, or ensoulment, took place until the "quickening" of the fetus. In modern times, until quite recently, the majority of Catholic theologians, following the biologists, identified conception with the moment of fertilization. But now consensus among biologists and physicians on this point no longer exists, and several leading Catholic theologians are changing their opinions.

The moment of ensoulment does not belong to the data of revelation. The bishops of Vatican Council II were aware of this when they composed their condemnation of abortion, which reads: "Therefore, from the moment of its conception, life must be guarded with the greatest care, while abortion and infanticide are unspeakable crimes."

This text in the *Pastoral Constitution on the Church in the Modern World,* before a final correction, referred to "life in the womb of the mother." A number of bishops argued that the expression "in the uterus" be deleted since the fertilized egg which is not in the uterus is "sacred." Others asked that a clearer description of abortion be made.

The commission correcting the text responded that the text should read simply "from the moment of conception" and pointed out that this explained the intention "without touching upon the moment of animation." The commission then stated that it could not give an accurate, technical definition of abortion, since the Church has no competence to settle the question of the precise moment when the fertilized ovum becomes a human being in the full sense, "for in this matter the Church must rely on the data of science and philosophical reflection."

We Catholics have strong arguments against abortion, but we weaken them when we make them depend upon an assumption that the human soul is present at the moment of fertilization.

ABORTION CASES

Q. *I had to have a therapeutic abortion. My two Catholic doctors told me I had no choice; it was my life for sure and little hope for the baby if the pregnancy continued. My husband agreed and I had it done in a non-Catholic hospital. I feel guilty about what I did, but it is even worse when I go to Sunday Mass and my husband doesn't go to Communion either because he feels he is guilty, too. What do we do? Must my husband confess it, too? And what do we do about the future? The children I already have need me. I must not get pregnant again. The doctors want me to use contraceptives.*

A.   The first thing you must both do is regain your peace of mind by making a good confession. It need not take long or require a lengthy discussion by the priest. Tell the priest you had an abortion performed and why. The "why" is most important for the fear of death and the insistence of the doctors most certainly lessened your moral guilt and may even have eliminated it altogether.

Then the two of you should seek the advice of an understanding priest, who will help you make a decision about the future. He cannot make the decision for you, but he can lay out for you the principles that will help you solve the moral dilemma you are in. Of one thing you can be sure: God does not want you to be terrified every time you make love. I have described these principles in a previous column (see pp. 160-162).

Q. *Is it true that if a person murders someone he can go to confession and receive absolution, yet a woman who has an abortion is excommunicated? Not that I believe in doing either, but if this is so, surely murder is murder and what is sauce for the goose is sauce for the gander.*

A. The woman who has an abortion can also go to confession and receive absolution if she is sorry for her action. It may seem odd to you that the penalty of excommunication is attached to the sin of abortion but not to other forms of murder. But there is a reason.

All men are agreed that other forms of murder are sinful. About abortion there is not this agreement. It is the Church that teaches abortion is sinful. By attaching the penalty of excommunication the Church adds emphasis to this teaching. If you are guilty of abortion, the Church says in effect, you reject the authority of the Church, you do not want to be in communion with it.

Q. *Many years ago I had a child out of wedlock. I rejected any suggestion made by anyone to have an abortion. I gave my little girl up for adoption. Two years later a young man and I were planning to marry, or so I thought. Again I became pregnant and one week before we were to marry he broke off and disappeared out of my life. I was desperate and panicked. My first pregnancy almost killed my parents. Within a few days I was in Mexico undergoing an abortion. Guilt-stricken, I went to confession and received absolution.*

I now have a wonderful husband and three lovely children. I try to keep close to God and receive the sacraments frequently. But I still become frightened at the destiny of my soul because of the horrible thing I have done. Will God have mercy on my soul even after what I have done? I am so ashamed.

A. You have God's own word for it that as a converted sinner you are someone he loves in a special way. Read the 15th chapter of Luke's gospel. There you will find Jesus' remarkable response to those who murmured against him. "This man receives sinners and eats with them." He described how God looks upon repentant sinners with three parables.

The first was about the shepherd who leaves the ninety-nine sheep to go after the one that was lost "until he finds it" and then calls in friends and neighbors to rejoice with him because he had found his sheep that was lost. The second was about the woman who lost her silver coin and searches diligently until she finds it and then calls to her neighbors: "Rejoice with me for I have found the coin which I had lost." From these Jesus makes the application to God: "Just so, I tell you, there is joy before the angels of God over one sinner who repents."

Then Jesus follows with the tremendous parable of the Prodigal Son, which might more rightly be called the Parable of the Loving Father. Pray over that story of the young man who demanded his inheritance, left home, squandered all in debauchery and then returned, hoping to become a hired hand on the family estate. Study the reaction of the father in the story who sees the lost son in the distance, rushes to him, embraces him, restores him to family honors and throws a great party in celebration. With the figure of the father Jesus is telling you how your heavenly Father looks upon you. When you returned to your father's house by confessing your sin, the Father restored you to all your Christian rights and honors. Keep on renewing your sorrow for what you did, keep on thanking God for going after you when you strayed, but don't question his mercy and love by doubting the sincerity of his pardon.

Having said this, I feel that I must say something about the nature of the sin you committed. You said that you panicked. Doubtless as you look back on it now, you must wonder how you did something so contrary to your moral convictions. It is quite possible that you were so carried away by your fears that you were not fully responsible for what you did. It may ease your mind to know that you may not have turned from God as completely as you thought you did. But whatever the sin, God assures you through scripture that he has forgotten it.

Q. *Could you tell me anything about the relatively new organization, Birthright, what it does, membership and volunteer requirements, etc.?*

A. Birthright is a program that offers alternatives to abortion. It is not an anti-abortion effort, not a lobbying organization. Check with your local Catholic Social Service office to find what form it takes in your city.

One of the features of the program is a telephone hotline through which girls in trouble may obtain information on how to get the proper counseling and what agencies will assist them. Volunteers are trained for this work. What motivates this movement is the conviction that it is not enough to be opposed to abortion, but that something positive must be done to afford an alternative to abortion.

Q. *This question has kept me up for many a night. I am a young Catholic girl who got herself pregnant a year ago. Since the boy I loved refused to marry me and to protect my family from shame, I had a legal abortion. Can I sincerely and sorrowfully repent of my sins and receive the sacraments? I am truly sorry.*

A. It is with God's help that you are sorry, and with his help you can now confess your sins and receive absolution. Don't put it off.

The mistake you made when you discovered your predicament was to go to the wrong person for advice. You should have asked the help of your parish priest who would have directed you to a home where you could have given birth to your baby and known that it would be adopted by a couple anxious for a child to love.

Q. *Many years ago I was very foolish to have an abortion, which at the time seemed a blessing until I fully realized the horror of it and have suffered very serious conscience pains. I went to confession and received absolution and have been receiving the sacraments regularly. Now that our bishops are reminding us that those Catholics who have abortions performed are excommunicated, I am a very unhappy old lady and much worried and wonder where I stand.*

A. You confessed your sin long ago and were forgiven. The forgiveness included absolution from any excommunication you might have incurred. Your letter is a lesson in itself that may keep others from making your mistake.

Q. *For 20 years I have lived with a hideous sin. At 17 I had an abortion, later married in a Catholic ceremony, without confessing. Lately it has engulfed me and I am remorseful, depressed and despairing. At last I have come to grips with the fact that, yes, it was I who did these monstrous things. I can stop blaming others. My question is: must I resign myself to the fact of eternal damnation or is there a way to be absolved? I must find absolution or I can't go on. How? Where?*

A. God has already touched you and shown his love for you. Only with the help of God can we recognize that we have done wrong and want to come back to him. God became man in Jesus for sinners and Jesus remains with us in his Church for sinners. You'll find him in his Church waiting to forgive you through the sacrament of Penance. The confessor is not going to condemn you or berate you. He is going to be happy you came to him. The most rewarding experience a priest has comes in the moments when he can help someone like you be reconciled with God. Go to any priest you know and open up to him.

NURSES, DOCTORS, CONGRESSMEN . . .

Q. *Should a Catholic nurse assist with an abortion if it is in her line of duty? I think not.*

A. I am sure that all who think it is wrong to procure an abortion would also hold that it is wrong to cooperate directly with someone else to do it. I say "directly" because there are surely some forms of cooperation that would not be wrong. The admittance clerk who registers a patient in the hospital for an abortion is cooperating in a way quite different from a nurse who assists the doctor in surgery who performs the act.

I think a Catholic nurse could give the usual pre-medication before operations or take charge of the patient in the recovery room in cases of abortion. This is routine care a nurse gives without giving the impression she agrees with what is being done to the patient. Even in surgery there may be some routine and less important tasks not directly concerned with the operation that a Catholic nurse could perform.

It is not possible to give a clear-cut, yes-or-no answer to all the problems a Catholic nurse will meet. The nurse herself will have to make the decision. For a rule of thumb she might ask herself: "Will what I do lead others to believe that my cooperation is an approval of what is going on?" Certainly a Catholic nurse should make known her opposition to direct abortion and ask to be excused from any immediate cooperation with the operation. Most hospitals will respect her conviction.

Q. *I saw your advice to nurses on abortion and thought you might be interested in copies of our guidelines for*

Catholic nurses in the abortion situation. The chaplains and directresses of nursing in all the hospitals of our archdiocese received copies of the enclosed guidelines. —Msgr. James G. Wilders, Director of the Hospital Apostolate, Archdiocese of New York.

A. Thank you, Msgr. Wilders. Your guidelines are most helpful. I am presuming you want them shared. Here is the portion that would be of general interest:

"Catholic doctors, nurses and ancillary staff are not to participate in any aspect immediately connected with the abortive procedure. 'Immediate connection' is understood to be that which is intimately and specifically involved with the abortion itself.

"It does NOT mean: normal pre- and postoperative care that would be given any patient, namely: 1) prepping, 2) medicating, 3) taking history, E.K.G., blood work, 4) preparing the instruments, preparing the operation room or any other place designated for the abortions. It does not mean: midwives or others who explain the routine procedures of abortion or channel the applicants to the proper persons. It does not mean witnessing the consent.

"It DOES mean: 1) the aborting physician, 2) his assistants, 3) scrub and circulating nurses, 4) the anesthetist."

Of general interest also is the reminder in the guidelines that the New York State hospital code includes the following provision for freedom of conscience: "No hospital employee or member of a medical staff shall be required by the hospital to participate in an abortional act who has notified the hospital of his decision not to participate in such act or acts." The guidelines recommend that Catholic personnel make this notification in writing.

The New York Bishops have had prepared "Guidelines for Action about the New York Abortion Law" which would be excellent help anywhere. Copies of this may be had by writing to the Hospital Apostolate, Archdiocese of New York, 65 East 89th Street, New York, N.Y. 10028.

Q. *All doctors and nurses and others who take part directly in an abortion are excommunicated from the Church. Does this apply to Justice Brennan, the only Catholic on the Supreme Court, who voted for the abortion bill?*

A. No, it does not. I personally think that the Supreme Court decision on abortion was atrocious and will destroy respect for life among our people — especially those who identify what is right or wrong with positive civil law. They are not the same, of course, and civil law cannot always outlaw and punish many moral evils. Until we learn otherwise, we must presume that Justice Brennan was not necessarily declaring himself in favor of abortion by his decision but merely agreeing with the majority of the Court that the U.S. Constitution does not allow laws prohibiting abortion in the first six months of pregnancy.

Q. *Is a person excommunicated for an abortion she had about 35 years ago, even though she has confessed it several times and was given absolution each time? I know she has been miserable all these years because of it and now she is more so with the threat of excommunication being published by the bishops.*

A. I answered this same question recently by pointing out that if such a person did incur excommunication, she was absolved from this when she received confessional absolution from sin. In response to this answer I received the following suggestion from a reader:

"I wish you had mentioned how valuable such a woman could be in right-to-life and birthright groups. An intelligent and articulate woman who has actually experienced the indignity of an induced abortion could be a very effective pro-life spokesman now. We need the testimony of these ladies, if they could just summon the courage to come forward. And if they still had unresolved guilt feelings (which they should not), maybe it would even help them feel better about it. It would take a considerable amount of courage, but for those who can afford the risk what a blessing it would be for them if they could dissuade just one other woman from destroying her unborn child."

Q. *Does the Church place any penalty or restriction on Catholic legislators who promote or vote for bills that legalize practices leading to abortion or euthanasia? Beyond this, is a Catholic legislator or official guilty of a serious sin if he makes no effort to oppose such legislation, or if they exist, isn't he compelled in conscience to work for the repeal of laws that are anti-life?*

A. The Church's penalty of excommunication applies only to those directly responsible for an immoral abortion. I do not know of any law concerning euthanasia, for this is something that is not yet a problem, though it soon may be. It is to be hoped that Catholics and all who oppose immoral abortions and attempts to introduce euthanasia will present a united front in working for laws that protect innocent life.

However, it is not always possible to eliminate immorality by law — especially when a majority of the citizens do not want the law. It is conceivable that a person who personally abhors the present practice of allowing abortion might conclude in good faith that when the majority of citizens want to make the option for abortion possible it is futile to work for new laws and better to spend one's energies trying to educate the people to the evils of easy abortion. There are Catholics who feel that it is impossible to obtain a constitutional amendment against abortion and that some other pro-life campaign should be conducted. We may disagree with them, but we have no right to condemn them.

Q. *If we, as Christians, believe that all life comes from God, if we agree the most important moment in life is the moment of conception and that God alone has the power over life and death and that in this way all men are equal, then why are we always instructed to leave the "God aspect" (if I may refer to God in this manner) out of our letters to congressmen when writing in reference to the abortion issue or euthanasia?*

A. You have reference, I believe, to the campaign to convince Congress that the United States should protect the right to life of the unborn. In a pluralistic society not all people base this right upon the same grounds. Atheists support the right to life and freedom but not on religious principles. Our only hope for success in this campaign is to keep from engaging in religious arguments, in making the pro-life movement appear to be a struggle between those who believe in God and those who do not.

We must build upon common ground — our common conviction that the right to life must be safeguarded. We must strive, therefore, to persuade congressmen that when the life of the most helpless of humans, the baby in the womb, is not protected, the right to life of all men is thereby weakened.

part 6

Divorce

Divorce

INDISSOLUBILITY

Q. *Lately on TV someone told me he heard that divorced Catholics could remarry in the Roman Catholic Church. That there was a new law passed concerning this.*

A. I know of no such new law. There has been some discussion in theological journals lately about the practice of the Orthodox Church of allowing remarriage after divorce in certain limited cases and the possibility of our Church changing its laws to conform with these in case there would ever be a reunion of the churches. Historians are now pointing out that the Council of Trent did not close the door to the possibility of some change in the Church's attitude toward the indissolubility of marriage, precisely because the council did not want to condemn the Orthodox practice. But for practical purposes our laws have not changed.

Q. *Well, here I am divorced 32 years, held on to my faith, Communion regularly. A good Catholic, and what happens? Changes in the Catholic faith that are unbelievable. Now they're talking about married priests. How about changing the rules on divorce? I am in the clear, but that does not help a lonely man of 62. How about a proper answer? I'm ready to give up my faith.*

A. Celibacy for priests is a Church law. What the Church made the Church can change. But the indissolubility of marriage is considered a law established by Christ himself. A law of this kind the Church considers itself powerless to change.

This may be the "proper" answer, but I am sure it does not satisfy you. What you want to know is whether with all the new thinking in the Church anyone is asking questions about people in your situation. You are not being forgotten.

Though the indissolubility of marriage may be something the Church cannot change, there is room for discussion about what makes a marriage indissoluble. In the past the Church has dissolved marriages contracted by exchange of vows but not physically consummated. The consummation was considered necessary to make the vows indissoluble. Some canonists, or church lawyers, today are arguing that the old concept of consummation was inadequate, that since man is an intelligent being capable of love, it would take more than a mere biological act to consummate a marriage.

Some marriages seem doomed from the start. One or both of the spouses never accept the responsibilities of marriage, never truly give a meaning to the vows exchanged, never respond to the other intelligently and lovingly. Are such marriages really consummated? The Church might decide someday they are not and therefore dissolve them so that the parties could enter a more serious union.

Your marriage did not last very long. Perhaps it fits the description I have given. If so, don't count on any immediate relief. The proposal for broadening the notion of consummation is merely in the talking stage. But then, the same is true about celibacy and the priesthood. So hang on, don't give up now.

Q. *In Matthew 19:9 it seems to me that Christ himself allows remarriage—if one's spouse has been unfaithful: "And I say to you: whoever divorces his wife, except for unchastity, and marries another, commits adultery." The parenthetical phrase, "except for unchastity," means, as I read it, one may not put away a spouse and marry another except in the case of unfaithfulness. Why does the Church ignore those words of Christ and teach something more strict than Christ himself?*

A. If you will read Mark 10:2-12, you will find what scripture scholars are agreed must have been Jesus' own clear stand against the possibility of marriage after divorce: "What therefore God has joined together let no man put asunder," and "Whoever divorces his wife and marries another commits adultery against her; and if she divorces her husband and marries another, she commits adultery."

Some scripture scholars believe that Matthew's parenthetical phrase represents an addition made by the early Church to Jesus' words. The Protestant *Interpreter's One-Volume Commentary,* holding that Mark 10 "was surely the teaching of Jesus himself," comments on Matthew 19:9 as follows: "Matthew shows that the early Church was not able to live by the radical demands of Jesus, but had instead to modify them in order to render them — as it thought — practicable."

The Gospel of Matthew was composed much later than Mark and does reflect a development in the thinking of the early Church and contains additions to the words of Jesus. However, the Christian writings other than scriptural of the first and second centuries indicate the early Christians were opposed to divorce for any reason. Several of the later Greek Fathers of the Church did accept Matthew's parenthetical phrase as allowing an exception and this explains how the Orthodox Church came to allow marriage after divorce in the case of adultery.

The Latin Fathers felt that Matthew's exception was so out of harmony with Mark and also Luke, whose gospel knows nothing of the exception, that they concluded the most it could mean was that a man might divorce his wife because of adultery but that this would not free either to marry again.

Q. *When is the Church going to change its antiquated marriage laws? Take the case of a good Catholic woman whose husband walks out on her and later remarries. She has done nothing wrong but she is not allowed to receive the sacraments, and as long as her husband is alive she cannot marry and is doomed to a life of loneliness. Yet an ex-nun, who of her own volition renounces her vows, may marry in the Church with the Church's blessing. Is that fair?*

A. I suppose every Catholic at times feels the way you

do about the Church's stand on marriage — particularly now that some priests and nuns are being released from their obligations and allowed to marry. I intend to discuss this problem seriously and honestly, but first I must clear up a few misunderstandings.

A woman whose husband divorces her may continue to receive the sacraments so long as she does not attempt another marriage. In fact, she is encouraged by the Church to do so often so that she may receive the grace to live a rich and meaningful life apart from marriage. Not all divorced persons are lonely and unhappy. Some prefer to remain as they are rather than risk another unhappy union.

A nun who "renounces" her vows is not free to marry "with the Church's blessing." She must take her vows seriously and petition the Church for a dispensation from them and abide by the decision of the Church before she is free to marry. But why and how does the Church release nuns from their vows and claim she is unable to release married people from theirs? Because she considers the religious or celibate state, and the vows and promises pertaining to them, something she herself created, whereas she holds marriage to be a state created by God. The Church releases people from her own laws, such as that forbidding meat on Fridays, but cannot dispense from God's law forbidding murder. Since the Roman Catholic Church has long held that Christ himself determined that marriage vows between Christians were to be permanent and indissoluble, she has considered this a law of God she could not dispense from.

All this sounds logical and clear in a theology classroom, but it can create misery and seeming injustices in the world in which we live. I do not see how the Church can go back on her teaching that Christian marriage is indissoluble, but I do see great possibilities of change from exploring more deeply what constitutes a Christian marriage.

What is this Christian marriage that is indissoluble? It is the union in Christ of two persons capable of living together as man and wife. In the case where it is impossible for a couple to perform the marriage act with each other, there is no marriage. Our church courts declare such unions invalid. But marriage is a union of persons not just of bodies. Is it possible that certain types of men and women are incapable of loving one another and living together for any length of time as man and wife? I think it is. We all know couples whose marriages ended in divorce after four or five stormy years and who subsequently entered second unions that were happy and successful. Is the union between two baptized incompatibles a real Christian marriage? That is the question the Church can pursue further and maybe answer in the negative without compromising her stand on the indissolubility of marriage.

Already church courts are declaring invalid marriages in which one of the parties is judged by psychiatrists to be psychologically incapable of making the permanent commitment of self necessary to meet the requirements of the Catholic notion of marriage. What of the chronic alcoholic who seems incapable of accepting the obligations and responsibilities of marriage, could he be declared incapable of entering a Christian marriage? Here's another question that needs exploring.

These are some of the possibilities for change in the Church's laws on marriage. But I would be less than honest if I did not warn you that they have not yet come about and may indeed never be acceptable. Church authorities move cautiously and gradually in these matters, for they are aware that the Church is one of the few institutions remaining that seriously promotes and defends the permanency of marriage. Many are, at the same time, acutely conscious of the misery and injustices some Catholics suffer from matrimonial tragedies. They are encouraging church lawyers and matrimonial courts to expand and clarify what constitutes a true Christian marriage.

Q. *A young couple who is very dear to us was divorced after a marriage in the Catholic Church and the birth of a child. Shortly after, they decided to come back together—for the sake of the child and because they realized their mistake. They were remarried by a judge, thinking they could not be remarried in the Catholic Church. Now there is a baby due and she will have to have it by Caesarean section. She would like to receive the sacraments before going into surgery. Does she lose all privileges after being divorced and remarrying the same person?*

A. As far as the Church is concerned the couple remained married after the divorce; by coming back together they did what was right. As far as the state is concerned, however, a remarriage is required. Normally in situations such as this — and they are quite common — the couple obtains a license and renews their marriage vows before a priest.

Your friends have no problem. If the woman obtained a divorce without permission of the Church and knew that this was wrong or thought she did wrong by remarrying before a judge she should confess before receiving Communion, but there is nothing more for her to do.

DIVORCE AND REMARRIAGE

Q. *Why were Catholic spokesmen so hesitant about saying anything definite concerning the marriage of Jacqueline Kennedy and the late Aristotle Onassis? Whether Onassis was free to marry or not, the marriage was invalid because it was not according to the Catholic form to which Mrs. Kennedy was bound. Why should her case be different from any poor little girl who marries outside the Church?*

A. The Onassis wedding raised questions most of us Catholics had not discussed before. In February, 1967, Rome changed her laws regulating marriages between Roman Catholics and the Orthodox. A decree of the Congregation for the Oriental Church permits bishops to dispense a Catholic of the Latin Rite from the obligation of observing the Catholic form of the marriage ceremony to be married in an Orthodox ceremony. But what is more, the decree states that if a Catholic marries an Orthodox in an Orthodox ceremony even without permission and a dispensation from a bishop, the marriage is valid. It would be disobedient and illicit to do this, but the marriage would be valid.

The decree declares that for a marriage between a Roman Catholic and an Orthodox "the presence of a sacred minister suffices for validity, presuming the other requisites of law are observed." In the Onassis wedding there seems to have been another requisite not observed, namely: the freedom to marry of the man.

The Orthodox Church recognizes divorce and freedom to marry again on the grounds of adultery. The Roman Catholic Church does not. Does the Roman Catholic Church recognize the power of the Orthodox Church to declare Onassis free to marry again? The Vatican press spokesman, Msgr. Fausto Vallainc, says it does not and implies thereby that Jacqueline is not validly married to Onassis. There may be, however, church lawyers and theologians who have doubts about Vallainc's conclusion.

Rome is making great efforts for unity with the Orthodox. The recognition of the validity of a marriage of a Roman Catholic in an Orthodox church was one more step toward that unity. Vatican Council II's *Decree on Ecumenism,* without hesitancy, recognized that the Orthodox Churches "possess true sacraments, above all — by Apostolic succession — the priesthood and the Eucharist" and "solemnly" declared that "the Churches of the East . . . have the power to govern themselves according to their own disciplines" (Par. 16). Could you argue from this that to be consistent Rome would have to recognize a divorce granted by an Orthodox Church? Maybe, particularly since at the Council of Florence in the 15th century, when the Eastern and Western Churches joined together for a brief time, no demands were made upon the Orthodox to give up their practice of divorce on the grounds of adultery.

Do you see now why some Catholic spokesmen were hesitant about saying anything definite about the Onassis marriage?

Q. *My husband and I have been deeply troubled since*

we watched a news program on television. We saw Mrs. Onassis receiving Communion at a Memorial Mass for Robert Kennedy. We realize there have been many changes in our Church, but surely not to this extent where a person who married a divorced man can receive the sacraments. Please do not ask "charity," as Cardinal Cushing did. I am not judging Mrs. Onassis. Simply tell us if there is a double standard for the rich and the poor. If there is, what kind of a church has this become?

A. I shall not ask for charity but for patience and calmness as we try to discuss a delicate and difficult problem that has upset not only you but thousands of other Catholics, if what the press reports is true.

Let's begin by making sure we agree upon the facts. No authorities of the Catholic Church invited Mrs. Jacqueline Onassis to receive Communion at the Memorial Mass for her brother-in-law, Robert Kennedy. The pastor in charge of the Mass, the Rev. Albert F. Pereira, has made it clear that there was no prior discussion or understanding with Mrs. Onassis.

"She walked up to the priest," Father Pereira explained, "he didn't go to her." And then he added something with which I think any priest would be in complete agreement: "No priest would under the circumstances pass her up and not give her Communion." How could he? To do so would be to set himself up as a self-appointed judge making a snap judgment in a matter about which he could not possibly have all the necessary information and creating a scene that might very well have made the Church look ridiculous before a television audience. Put yourself in the position of the priest giving Communion and ask yourself what you would have done.

But you may legitimately ask: "Why do not the authorities of the Church now publicly state that Mrs. Onassis, married to a divorced man as she is, has no right to receive the sacraments in the Catholic Church?" Here we expose the delicate nature of the problem. Jacqueline Kennedy married a divorced man all right, but he was a divorced man that the Orthodox Church declared free to remarry.

The Roman Catholic Church permits certain divorced persons to remarry in cases where she declares the previous marriages invalid for some reason or other, or dissolves a marriage in favor of the faith, as we say, in which one of the parties was not baptized (the Pauline Privilege) or dissolves a marriage between two baptized persons which was not consummated after the wedding ceremony.

The Orthodox Church officially declared the divorced Mr. Onassis free to marry and authorized his marriage with Jacqueline Kennedy. Any attempt by our Church to declare that marriage invalid could be construed as an insult to the Orthodox.

We Roman Catholics find ourselves in an ambiguous position in regard to marriages with the Orthodox. Our Church now recognizes as valid a marriage between a Roman Catholic and an Orthodox in an Orthodox church, even without the presence of a Catholic priest or any authorization from a Catholic bishop. Catholics may now be dispensed from the Catholic form of marriage to contract marriage validly in a Protestant Church, but such a dispensation presumably would not be granted unless the bishop were sure the Protestant party was free to marry according to Catholic regulations. The situation with the Orthodox Church is different.

Our Church now recognizes officially that the Orthodox have apostolic succession of orders and the power to make their own church law. In the Decree on Ecumenism, Vatican Council II solemnly declared that "the Churches of the East, while keeping in mind the necessary unity of the whole Church, have the power to govern themselves according to their own disciplines, since these are better suited to the temperament of their faithful and better adapted to foster the good of souls. Although it has not always been honored, the strict observance of this traditional principle is among the prerequisites for any restoration of unity" *(Decree on Ecumenism,* No. 16).

To be consistent, therefore, it would seem that our Church must recognize a divorce granted by an Orthodox Church to one of its members. By divorce the Orthodox in many instances means what our Church calls a declaration of nullity. But it can also mean a dissolution of a marriage bond in favor of the innocent party in a case of adultery or desertion.

The Eastern Church has observed this practice from the earliest days of Christianity. And it is important to note that in the 15th century at the Council of Florence, when the Eastern and Western Churches were briefly reunited, no stipulation was required by the Latin Church that the East give up this practice of remarriage after divorce on the grounds of adultery.

So, the case of Mrs. Onassis is not as simple as it may seem. She is not receiving any special consideration because of her wealth or prominence. But the fact that she is who she is does put the spotlight on an ecumenical problem that, to say the least, deserves consideration by our church leaders and scholars.

Q. *My friend has a marriage problem. Gerry, a Southern Baptist, married a man of the same religion in a Southern Baptist church. They were only married three months and they divorced. Then Gerry married a Catholic man before a justice of the peace. They have two children.*

Gerry began taking instructions to become a Catholic and wants to be married in the Church. But here's the problem. The local Catholic matrimonial court says she can't become a Catholic because her first husband is alive and we recognize their church. Now I have been a Catholic all my life and I never knew that the Catholic Church would recognize this faith. Does it? I know Gerry is very sincere about becoming a Catholic. I feel sorry for her. Can you tell us where to turn, please?

A. I suppose that what your friend was told was that the Catholic Church recognizes as valid the marriage that took place in the Baptist Church. It is a rather common mistake among Catholics to assume that our Church does not consider permanent the marriages contracted in other churches or before civil authorities. There are several reasons for this.

First, because Catholics who are bound to the Catholic form of marriage are not considered to be married in the eyes of the Church if they contract a civil marriage in another church or before civil authorities. And second, because some marriages contracted by those not members of our Church can be dissolved by a subsequent marriage in the Catholic Church.

Our Church considers sacramental, and therefore indissoluble, only those marriages in which both the man
and woman are baptized. When one or both parties are
not baptized, the marriage is considered merely a natural
bond that can be dissolved in favor of the party wishing
to embrace the faith.

Evidently your friend and her first husband had been
both baptized at the time they were married in the Baptist
Church. In such a case theirs was a sacramental and indissoluble marriage — they received the sacrament of
Matrimony according to our Catholic thinking — even
though not aware of our Catholic understanding of it.

The fact that the marriage lasted only three months,
however, suggests that there might have been something
lacking in the marriage consent. If they had no serious
intention of remaining together, if they married only to
give a baby a name with the intention of separating, there
may have been no true marriage. You may have your
friend look into this in case the marriage court has not
already done so.

Urge your friend to continue her instructions in the
faith so that she can help bring up her children as Catholics. She and her husband should go to Mass with the
children and be as active in parish life as they can be
under the circumstances.

Q. *Would you cast your vote for a presidential candidate who had been divorced and remarried? I say a
man running for public office should be judged solely
upon his political ability and past performance. My wife
says it would be a scandal to the world to have a remarried divorced man in the White House, since the*

President is not only a political leader but a symbol of the United States.

A. It seems to me that it is primarily as a political leader, not as a family man that the President is a symbol of the United States. In a presidential election we are not choosing the "father of the year."

I might be very unhappy about the marital status of a given candidate, but if I thought he showed better balance in political decision-making, more ability to inspire confidence for unity at home and cooperation with other nations, and offered more hope of ending war than a candidate who would be a better symbol of family life, I'd vote for him without any hesitancy.

Q. *I would like to know if I could marry in a Catholic Church a non-Catholic man who was married in a non-Catholic Church and who is divorced but has never been baptized?*

A. The marriage of two unbaptized persons or the marriage of a baptized and a non-baptized person is considered by the Church to be a "natural bond union," that is, a non-sacramental union. Holy and serious though it is, such a union may under certain conditions be dissolved by the Church.

I can only advise you to see your pastor and give him all the known facts of the first marriage. He will then determine what steps you must take.

Q. *I am a Catholic, 53 years old, never married. I am interested in a woman, not a Catholic, who was twice married. Her first husband disappeared about a year after they were married. This was some 20 years ago.*

Neither she nor his relatives have heard a word from him or anything about him in all this time. She married again and her second husband died. Does our Church law still consider her married to her first husband and would it be wrong for me to date this lady?

A. You have waited so long it would be a great pity now to enter a marriage that might keep you from the sacraments. Before you get too deeply involved with this woman, you should discuss her case with your parish priest. It is quite possible that she may be free to marry. Her first husband may be dead.

It is not always necessary to prove the death of the other party to establish freedom to marry. Circumstances surrounding the disappearance, the health of the person, his attitude toward family and relatives, the type of work he engaged in, all could be the basis of a presumption that he had died. The mere fact of his disappearance without any trace, however, is not in itself sufficient basis for such a presumption. The facts in the case should be submitted to your local bishop. If he considers the circumstantial evidence sufficient to create a moral certainty of the death, he will give permission for your marriage to the woman.

Q. *I am a Catholic and I would like to know if it is permissible for me to marry in the Catholic Church a man who is divorced but has never been baptized?*

A. The chances are that you may receive permission. If one of the parties to the marriage was not baptized, then the marriage was not sacramental and therefore can be dissolved. Go see your pastor and ask for direction.

Q. *My daughter was raised a Catholic. She was married at 16, under duress, by a priest. She was divorced after three years, during which time another child was born. Also during this time, her husband was jailed several times for being drunk in a public place and gambling. Later I found he had been married to another Catholic girl under the same circumstances, except this time not by a priest. He deserted her right after the baby was born.*

My two grandchildren are now five and six years old. They need a father and my daughter is considering getting married again. She knows she cannot remain in the Church if she does so; her pastor told her nothing could be done about her first marriage. So she has started sending the children to an Episcopal Sunday school and attending some of the services herself. Here are two cases almost identical. One had the misfortune of being married by a priest so she and her children are being lost to the Church; the other is being welcomed back into the fold and is free to marry again. Is this fair?

A. Your daughter need not be lost to the Church. She should discuss her case with the matrimonial court of the diocese she lives in. If she was married "under duress," the marriage may have been invalid on that score; if what you say about the man can be substantiated it may be possible to prove that he had no serious intentions of being married. Our Church courts are more willing to consider cases on these grounds than before.

Q. *I am a recent widow. I miss my husband physically, emotionally and intellectually. I would like to remarry.*

*But whom? I have two good male friends that I feel
strongly for and they both would like to marry me. They
are divorced. At age 40 is there any hope I can find
someone who is eligible in the eyes of the Church? A
dropout priest? Or a widower? Not too probable. I am
racked up by my conscience and feel it is not human to
reject two beautiful relationships—potentially permanent—because of their past. I do not choose to be
celibate. Must I be? I need a theological opinion.*

A. Be patient, sister, If you have two men on the string
in so short a time, you obviously won't have too much
trouble landing an eligible bachelor or widower. Keep
on fishing. But leave the priests alone unless you are
sure they are already dropouts. Priests are having
troubles enough these days without lonely widows setting
traps for them.

It is not a theological opinion you need, but a few
blunt words of advice. You should be grateful. It is evident that you were blessed with a good husband. That is
more than many women ever enjoy. Show your gratitude
now by helping others to some happiness. There are
other widows and widowers experiencing your same
problems. Look for them. And if there is no social
organization for such persons, organize one. I know
of one such organization that was the result of a letter
to the editor of a diocesan paper inviting interested
parties to meet after a specified Mass in front of a
centrally located church.

What I am trying to say is, don't be in such a hurry
to throw your heart and your religion away. You haven't
yet exhausted the possibilities.

Q. *A Catholic man divorced his Catholic wife of ten years. He had no grounds, and, even though she did, she did not contest because he promised to remarry her later if she would not contest it. Now he is planning on returning home to live with her in the meantime. She thinks this is all right since they were originally married in the Church and divorce is not recognized by her religion. What do you think?*

A.   You arouse my curiosity. Why would he divorce her with the promise to remarry her? Tell us more. It is true that the Church still considers this couple married and they would be guilty of no moral wrong by living together. But they are not legally married, and she would have no legal protection whatsoever. So if she is smart she'll insist upon a trip to the courthouse for a license.

Q. *The girl I am engaged to has been divorced for two years. She is Protestant, baptized and was married by a minister. However, her former husband was previously married, also by a minister. I have been told by a friend that her marriage is not valid and, therefore, we can be married in the Catholic Church. Is this correct?*

A.   It may be, if you can establish the fact that the first wife of the man was living at the time he married the girl you are engaged to. It must be shown that this first marriage was a true marriage and not invalid for some reason or other. You should talk this over with a priest.

What you will need for proof is a certified copy of the court record of the man's first marriage and also a copy of the questionnaire filled out by this couple when

they applied for their marriage license. From this it can
be discovered whether this first wife had ever been
married before and also whether both were of sufficient
age.

Q. *To settle a friendly argument, please answer this
question: Can a Protestant boy, one month after his
divorce, marry a Catholic girl in the Catholic Church at
a nuptial Mass?*

A. Yes, if the Church declared his marriage invalid or
declared that he was free to make use of the Pauline
Privilege, by which a marriage between persons not baptized may be dissolved in favor of the faith. The girl he
previously married may have been married before. Or
the marriage could have been invalid for other reasons,
e.g., she may have entered the marriage with the intention of having no children or only one child, or he
or she may not have entered the marriage freely. We
would presume that the Church investigations of the
marriage were going on while the divorce proceedings
were in progress.

Q. *A man who was baptized a Catholic but not brought
up in the faith married a non-Catholic woman before a
minister or justice of the peace. The marriage ended in
divorce. Is the man, as a baptized Catholic, free to
marry a Catholic in the Church?*

A. It is difficult to answer questions like this concerning
the validity of marriage without a personal interview
with the parties concerned. Were both the parents of the
man Catholic or one or both of them Protestants?

When did the marriage take place? These are some of the questions that need to be answered.

If the man's parents were both Catholic, then he was bound to the Catholic form of marriage; his civil marriage would be considered invalid according to church law and he is free to marry in the Catholic Church. If one or both his parents were not Catholic and he had no Catholic upbringing whatsoever, then before 1949 he was not bound to the Catholic form of màrriage; after 1949 he was bound to it. So, if he was married before January 1, 1949, he is not free to marry — unless there are other reasons why the marriage was not valid: if after January 1, 1949, he is free to marry. Complicated? From January 1, 1949, the Church's law regarding the form of marriage was changed to make it apply to anyone baptized as a Catholic, whether his parents were Catholic or not, whether he was brought up as a Catholic or not. This was done to simplify the law. Before the change it was difficult to decide what constituted Catholic upbringing.

Q. *My husband, a Protestant, has instigated divorce proceedings against me on the grounds of desertion and cruel and abusive treatment. Because these statements are untrue I am contesting the divorce. Everybody seems surprised at this: because he wants the divorce everyone seems to think I should let him have it.*

My lawyer wants me to sue for the divorce; he argues that my husband can always go into another state and obtain his freedom, that I cannot follow him around forever contesting a divorce. I have tried to talk to a priest about this, and before I even discussed the case fully with him he called the chancery and obtained permission for me to obtain the divorce. My lawyer keeps pleading with me: "Seek the divorce; he is not going to live with you." Even so, just because he is not going to live with me does that entitle him to a divorce? I have found out that divorce proceedings are a farce; I told my lawyer so, and he agreed.

With all the changes in attitude of the Catholic Church today, I would like to know whether or not my religion is backing me.

A.   Your Church does, indeed, back you in your strong opposition to divorce. But in a country in which, as your lawyer pointed out, your husband will eventually get a divorce, you may be obliged to countersue to protect your interests. That's why the Church authorities have given you permission to go ahead. This permission does not mean that you will be free to marry again as far as the Church is concerned. You can give witness to the Church's stand on the permanency of marriage by not attempting marriage again after the divorce.

Q.   *A non-Catholic couple was married and at the time of the wedding the bride had never been baptized. Some time later she decided to be baptized in a non-Catholic church. After several years, the couple divorced. Eventually the man married a Catholic girl. Is there any way by which such a marriage can be righted in the eyes of the Catholic Church?*

A.   There is no possibility of dissolving the marriage in favor of the faith by using what is known as the Pauline Privilege, if that is what you want to know. Whether or not the marriage was invalid for some reason or other must be discussed with your parish priest. I hope it is clear in your mind that a marriage between two baptized Protestants is considered by the Catholic Church just as indissoluble as a marriage between two Catholics.

Q. *What are the circumstances under which a Catholic may marry a Protestant who has been divorced?*

A. This is a question that cannot be answered satis-factorily here. In general it can be said that the Catholic Church looks upon the marriages of Protestants as she does those between Catholics. If the Protestants were baptized, neither previously married and both freely intended to enter a lifelong union with no agreements not to have children, then they are in a sacramental mar-riage as indissoluble as a marriage of two Roman Catholics performed by a bishop.

So the question you ask about a divorced Protestant is the same you ask about a divorced Catholic: Are there any reasons for thinking that the first marriage was in-valid? There are many, of which these are the principal:

Did one or both the parties refuse the right to have children, even temporarily? Did one of the parties enter marriage with the intention of getting a divorce if it did not work out? Did the first spouse suffer from personality problems so severe he could not commit himself to the permanency of marriage? Was either forced into the marriage? Was the first spouse incapable of heterosexual love? Or impotent?

In the case of a divorced Catholic we ask whether or not the marriage took place in the Church, for the Catholic can only be validly married when he observes the rules of his Church. These do not apply to Protestants except indirectly. If the divorced Protestant was married to a Catholic or a fallen-away Catholic in a Protestant church or before a justice of the peace, then the marriage would be considered invalid because of the Catholic party's failure. In the case of the divorced Protestant we also ask whether one or the other of the parties might be unbaptized, for if so there may be a possibility of dissolving the marriage in favor of the faith.

This does not exhaust the possibilities, but this should be enough to make it clear that if your question is more than hypothetical, you should discuss your case with a priest who will either help you or refer you to the proper authorities. Do not decide that your situation fits one of the circumstances listed here and go on dating a divorced person.

Q. *Isn't it true that a person baptized as an adult is not held responsible for his deeds prior to baptism? Would this include marriage to a divorced woman?*

A. The sacrament of Baptism forgives all sins committed prior to baptism, but it does not in any way release a person from moral obligations rising from contracts, family and business obligations, etc. A man who stole $5,000 before his baptism would be forgiven the sin committed if he had the proper sorrow at the time of baptism, but he still would be obliged to return the stolen money.

If you are asking whether baptism in the Catholic Church would make the man's marriage to the divorced woman acceptable in the Church, then the answer is no. If he has left the divorced woman, he can be accepted in the Church, and by proving that the woman had a living husband at the time he married her, he may be declared free to marry again in the Church.

Q. *An intelligent 27-year-old man who graduated from Catholic grade and high school is engaged to a Protestant girl. She had been married at 18 to a Protestant, separated and divorced at 19. She is now 24, mature, considerate and with the personality and qualities parents want in the wife of their son. We all would like to know if there is any possibility of having a priest officiate with the minister at their wedding.*

A. The fact that the girl's marriage ended with divorce so soon suggests that her union may have been invalid. The man may have entered the marriage without any serious intention of binding himself permanently; he may have refused to have children; there are all sorts of possibilities. Urge your son to discuss this case with a priest.

Q. *Recently my son came home and told me that he planned to marry a divorced woman. Now he says that he spoke to a priest and that he will not be excommunicated and will still be able to receive the sacraments. How can this be possible?*

A. Evidently the woman's first marriage was invalid for some reason or other. Perhaps the husband she divorced had been previously married, or maybe he was a Catholic and they were not married according to the Catholic form of marriage necessary for validity. There could be other reasons why her marriage was invalid. You need more information from your son.

Q. *Should I send anniversary cards to relatives who had been married in the Church, got divorced and then married in Protestant churches? Is the Church condoning these marriages by saying it's OK, "they're in the family"?*

A. No, the Church does not condone those second marriages. We Catholics, however, may sympathize with friends and relatives whose marriages fail and find it impossible to live alone. We should befriend them and help them any way we can. But I can't see any point in sending them anniversary cards; we certainly shouldn't want to congratulate them for what they did.

Q. *How is it possible for a divorced man with children to be married in a Catholic church?*

A. There are all sorts of possibilities. Maybe his wife was a divorced woman when he married her. Maybe, by the way she acted after the marriage, she demonstrated that she never intended to be serious about her marriage obligations. Maybe he or the woman was a Catholic, bound to the Catholic form of marriage, and they were married, as we say, outside the Church, in which case if the union was never validated by the Church, he was free to marry in the Church to another woman.

There are other possibilities, but to mention them would require lengthy explanations to avoid misunderstandings. In cases of this kind the proper thing to do is to inquire at the parish where the marriage took place.

Q. *With all the changes in the Church, can a Catholic*

*girl receive Communion now even though she was
married in a Lutheran church four years ago, because
the priest refused since the groom had been previously
married and divorced?*

A. The Church's teaching on the permanency of marriage has not changed, though the grounds of nullity
have been extended in some instances. The woman
should not receive until she can rectify her marriage. It
may be possible to prove that her husband's first marriage
was invalid. She should discuss her problem with a priest
who can help her explain the details of the first marriage
to the church matrimonial court in her diocese.

Q. *I divorced many years ago and remarried. However,
I lived a very short time as man and wife with my
second husband. My conscience bothered me and I
wanted to take part in every phase of my faith. My first
husband has since died, but I am still living apart in the
same house with my second husband. Does the Church
now allow us to live as man and wife, or do we have to
have a religious ceremony? My husband is non-Catholic
and doesn't think this necessary.*

A. Tell your husband that all you need to do is renew
your marriage vows before a priest and two witnesses.
Go see your priest. He will obtain the proper dispensations and have you renew your vows in a simple ceremony. Even if your husband refuses to renew the vows
this way, the priest can obtain a rectification of your
marriage through the bishop, so long as you are sure
your husband intends to continue living with you.

Q. *I have a Catholic friend who married a divorcee. He says "they will have their marriage blessed." They were married by a judge. Does our Church bless a person married to a divorcee?*

A. Your friend evidently has hopes that his civil marriage can be rectified. If this happens it can only be possible because the previous marriage of the divorcee was invalid or can be dissolved in favor of the faith. A marriage that is not sacramental and therefore a symbol of the union between Christ and the Church — i.e., a marriage between unbaptized persons or a union in which one party is not baptized — is not considered indissoluble by the Church. Such a marriage may be dissolved by a subsequent marriage in the Church so that the Catholic party may practice the faith. If both parties to the first marriage were upbaptized and one party became a Catholic, he or she may be given permission by the local bishop to make use of what is known as the Pauline Privilege. If one party was baptized, then permission must be obtained from Rome. This is considered an extension of the Pauline Privilege.

Q. *My sister is marrying a divorced man in a Protestant church. She was divorced from her husband last summer. My sister and her former husband are Catholic and were married in a Catholic church 26 years ago. My sister would like me to give her away at the wedding. Many years ago I was restricted by church law from being a best man for a buddy who was marrying a Protestant girl in a Protestant church. He was also Protestant. What does the Catholic Church teach today as far as my participation or attendance at my sister's wedding?*

A. Today you would be allowed to stand up for a Protestant buddy marrying another Protestant in a Protestant marriage. The case of your sister is another problem. She is not free to marry unless her first marriage and the first marriage of her intended are declared invalid. I presume this is not possible and that is why she is marrying in a Protestant ceremony. What she is doing is wrong. We will not judge her, for we know not what goes on in her mind. But for you to give her away would be a formal approval of what she is doing. You might decide that rather than offend her and cut her off, you should attend the wedding, but I would advise you to explain to her charitably that you do not feel you can in conscience take an active part.

Q. *I was married to a Catholic in the Church. I obtained a divorce without seeking permission from the bishop. What is my status in the Church?*

A. You are still in the Church, if you want to be, though you are not free to marry again unless your marriage can be declared invalid by the Church for some reason. If you did not know that you had an obligation to obtain permission from the bishop, then you, of course, were not disobedient and would not be guilty of sin. If you did know about the obligation and deliberately ignored it, you probably feel guilty and better talk the matter over with a confessor. Some dioceses may require that you sign a statement that you do not consider the divorce a permission to marry again.

Q. *A divorced Catholic who remarries cannot have the benefit of a priest to perform any kind of a ceremony, but the Church recognizes a Catholic marriage performed in a Lutheran church where our priest's presence wasn't even allowed. To me this adds insult to injury. I realize a divorced person isn't entitled to the Mass and a Catholic marriage, but why can't a priest perform some ceremony if the Church now sanctions a marriage in a Protestant church? This is not just or fair.*

A. You are mixing potatoes and shoes. If a divorced Catholic is unable to be married in the Church, that means the Church considers this particular person incapable of a valid marriage. No ceremony, civil or religious, can in any way change the situation in the eyes of the Church. It is not a matter of the divorced Catholic being punished by depriving him or her of the services of the priest. The person is not free to marry. A priest who would perform any kind of ceremony would be condoning something wrong.

In the other case, we presume that both the Catholic and the Protestant are free to marry. The Church in this case dispenses the Catholic party from the obligation to be married before a priest and two witnesses. For a great part of the history of the Church it was not necessary for a Catholic to be married in the presence of a priest.

Q. *Can a Catholic couple, both baptized and married in the Catholic Church by a priest, get a divorce and marry someone else in a few years because of desertion?*

A. Desertion alone does not allow the innocent party freedom to marry again. Desertion, however, might indicate there was something wrong with the marriage from the very beginning. It could mean that the one who broke up the marriage never intended to enter a permanent union, or never intended to be faithful, or was a sociopathic personality unable to cope with the intimacies and obligations of married life. All such cases as this should be discussed with a local priest who can discuss the possibilities or direct the person to the proper authorities.

SEPARATION

Q. *How would you classify the following: married, separated or divorced? Marriage took place more than 25 years ago, both Catholics. Husband left wife three years after marriage. Have not seen each other since. Wife would not consent to divorce at that time and doesn't intend to in the future.*

1) What is the status of each? 2) Any chance of reconciliation? 3) What are the legal entanglements of such a marriage, if any—if this is called a marriage? 4) If one is at fault for such an outcome, should the one not at fault have to suffer?

A. I would call them married people who are separated, wouldn't you? Certainly they are not divorced. Until they are legally divorced, the State, I imagine, would consider theirs a legal marriage. This might mean in some states that they are legally responsible for each other's debts and legal obligations. But don't ask me, ask a lawyer.

There is always a chance of reconciliation. The very fact that no divorce was obtained after all these years of separation would indicate that there is a good possibility of reconciliation. If the man really wanted the divorce he could have got it long ago even over the opposition of his wife. It looks to me as though both sides are at fault here.

Q. *I was married in the Catholic Church 16 years ago. Approximately three years ago I obtained a civil divorce. Knowing the Church's stand on divorce, I would like to know if my former husband and I were remarried, would a civil ceremony be acceptable to the Church, since the Catholic marriage would still be recognized by the Church as valid in spite of the divorce?*

A. A civil ceremony would be acceptable in this case. Civil law would require a remarriage and therefore some ceremony recognized by the State must be gone through even though the Catholic parties consider themselves already married in the eyes of God. It would seem preferable to renew your vows before a priest so that the Church is made aware of your intentions to live together again.

Q. *Now that we have so many changes and new rules, can a Catholic man or woman married in the Church and now divorced receive Holy Communion? There are a number of divorced Catholics that go to Mass that I know but say they cannot receive Holy Communion. Is this true?*

A. Catholics are obliged to seek permission from their

bishops to sue for civil divorce, and before this is granted they must agree that the civil action does not free them from the bonds of marriage so that they can marry again.

Once divorced under these conditions, they are free to receive the sacraments. A Catholic who obtained a divorce without permission may repent of his action, agree not to marry again and return to the sacraments. In both instances, it is presumed that a reconciliation is impossible and that the person is willing to resume life with the divorced spouse should circumstances change.

Q. *My husband has given me cause for divorce but because of our children and not wanting our married children to know of their father's infidelity I have done nothing legally. I always considered myself a warm and loving wife, but evidently my husband thought otherwise. He claims he still wants me and loves me. I have continued living with him as his wife and have asked God's help to forget but it just is not working. Is there any possible way to get a separation through the Church, as I do not want to give up my sacramental rights by divorce and I know my husband still wants to keep his religion?*

A. Provided you have first sought permission from the Church, you may obtain a divorce and still retain your sacramental rights. Separations do not always afford the proper legal protections and a divorce may be necessary. The divorce, of course, does not give you the right to marry again in the Church.

Talk your problem over with a parish priest. He may be able to help you forgive your husband and live the remaining years of your life in peace. Old age without a companion can be mighty lonely. You had better think twice about breaking up your marriage. If there is no other solution, the priest will help you obtain permission of the Church for a separation or divorce.

Q. *Why is it that when we marry we take a vow to live with our partner through sickness and health, etc., and yet so many women afterwards don't live with their husbands for some silly reason or other? Yet priests don't say a word to these people. I know, because a friend of mine did this and the parish priest knows all about it but doesn't say anything.*

A. Then he probably knows much more about the situation than you do. No mature, responsible adult would refuse to honor the vow of marriage because of "some silly reason or other." More than likely, if a couple is living apart and the wife is welcomed and recognized as an active participant in the parish, the priest knows there is some grave circumstance which prevents her living with her husband.

Friends do not always know the real causes for a separation, nor have they any right to know. A silly reason might be given to squelch the questions of the nosy.

Q. *The Church permits divorced people who remarry to receive the sacraments if they live together as brother and sister. Why then should a middle-aged person separated because of an intolerable situation having developed (no divorce or remarriage involved) be denied the sacraments while regularly attending Mass and otherwise observing church regulations?*

A. If there are serious reasons for the separation, then there is no reason why you should be denied the sacraments. If you are convinced that you have no choice other than the present arrangement, you are doing nothing sinful and need no one's permission to receive Communion.

ANNULMENTS

Q. *My wife, a non-Catholic, insists she knows of a divorced Catholic man who was married again in the Church while his first wife was still living. Is this possible?*

A. Yes, if the Church, in a decree of nullity, had declared the first marriage invalid for one reason or another. The divorce would be needed to satisfy civil or legal requirements if there were no legal annulment.

Q. *I would like to know if I could marry in the Catholic Church a Catholic man who was once married outside the Church to a non-Catholic by a judge. He was 17 and in the three years of marriage he lived six months with her and she left their little girl with him. His lawyer is trying to get him a divorce or an annulment.*

A. If the man were baptized a Catholic, he was subject to the law of the Catholic Church concerning the form of marriage. If, therefore, the marriage before the judge was not subsequently rectified before an authorized priest and two witnesses, then the man would be free to marry you in the Catholic Church once freed by divorce from his civil obligations. It will be necessary to have these facts investigated by the office of the bishop of your diocese which will issue a statement that the man is free to marry. So approach your pastor well before the time of marriage so that he can help you make the proper preparations.

Q. *The Church has opened its doors, so to speak, in so many aspects of our religion. Has anyone ever delved into the matter of marriage annulment? This, naturally, is of personal interest to me. The particular grounds being refusal of one party to have children.*

A. The Church has modernized her regulations so that marriage cases can be settled easier. Consequently our church courts were able to accept more petitions for annulment than before. You should present your case to your local tribunal. Your parish priest will tell you how to do it. If one party entered marriage with the intention of withholding the right to have children from the other, the marriage would be invalid.

Q. *My husband deserted me and my four children about 18 years ago. I haven't seen him or heard from him in all those years. The law of the State says after seven years if you haven't seen or heard from a person he is declared dead for purposes of marriage. Does this apply to the laws of the Church? If I considered marriage again, would I have any problems?*

A. The Church is stricter in this case than the State. The mere fact of disappearance without any trace is not considered sufficient proof of death by the Church, even though the person may have been unheard of for years.

But this does not mean that a death certificate is the only proof acceptable.

Your bishop can authorize you to marry again, if you furnish him with circumstantial evidence sufficient to create a moral certainty of the death of your husband. Can you show that not only you but his relatives and friends have not heard from him? Was his health bad? These are the questions you should discuss with a local priest who can help you present your case to the bishop. Such a case is not complicated; it does not require any formal trial, but merely the decision of the bishop.

Q. *Would you explain just how a person gets an annulment of a first marriage. What grounds must one have to obtain one and just whom should one talk to about it? I have known this young man for over four years. We were attracted to each other very strongly, but he is divorced. He received a divorce on the grounds of adultery. His wife deserted him and their child. He now has custody of his daughter and his wife does not have visiting rights. They were married by a Catholic priest and were both of age. She was not pregnant so they were not forced into marriage. From this brief story do you think he would have a chance to get an annulment?*

A. Yes, he has a chance. The fact that his wife deserted him and was judged by the courts to be a mother unfit even to visit her child indicates that she may not have made a serious commitment to marriage.

A person of this type may be so emotionally disturbed she is incapable of accepting responsibility and, therefore, incapable of committing herself to the serious, lifelong contract Catholics consider marriage to be.

You should discuss this case with one of your parish priests. He will either help you himself or direct you to a priest who specializes in marriage cases.

Q. *What is the Church's position on the annulment of a marriage where one of the spouses is insane?*

A. It all depends upon the kind of insanity. If the mental breakdown occurs some years after the wedding, it would not nullify the marriage any more than other serious sickness would. A couple takes each other "for better or for worse, in sickness and in health. . . ."

However, there are forms of insanity which render a person incapable of making the serious commitment of self required for a valid marriage. Persons afflicted in this way may be capable of holding a steady job, but they are unable to love others. Often the existence of this condition does not become known until the tensions of married life expose the basic weakness of the personality.

Our church courts make use of psychiatrists as experts in judging whether or not a marriage was null and void from the beginning because of insanity. In recent years the church courts have declared more marriages invalid on the grounds of insanity than previously, because modern psychiatry has discovered more about the aberrations of the human mind and how long a mental illness can influence a person's decisions before it manifests itself for what it is.

Q. *Our daughter, 24 years old, goes with a man who was divorced from his wife several years ago because she was running around with other men and wanted to be free. Our daughter says she can't give him up and will marry him. Which would be worse: to get married in court and attend Catholic services but be cut off from the sacraments or, what they consider doing, to join the Lutheran Church where they could practice that religion in full? They went to see a priest, but he said they cannot get an annulment of his first marriage because adultery is not grounds for annulment.*

A.   True, adultery may be grounds for divorce but it does not nullify a marriage that was valid in the beginning. However, adultery may be an indication that a marriage was invalid from the beginning because the adulterous party had no intentions of remaining faithful or looked upon marriage as something that need not be permanent. It is possible that the marriage of the man your daughter wants to marry may have been invalid for such reasons as these. She should pursue the investigation of the marriage further.

Your other question is a little more delicate. If your daughter believes that she is doing wrong in leaving the Catholic Church, then she will double the mistake by marrying in the Lutheran Church. Encourage her not to leave her Church even though she finds it impossible to live up to the Catholic ideal of marriage. She can continue to attend Mass and bring her children up in the faith and even take an active part in parish life in which her children are raised, as others do who find themselves in similar situations.

Q.   *A friend of mine left the Catholic religion and joined a Protestant church and got married in that church. Then about 15 years later his wife divorced him and he returned to the Catholic Church. Can he remarry in the Catholic Church and receive the sacraments?*

A. Yes, he can. Before he may marry again, however, he needs a declaration of the nullity of his marriage in the Protestant church. This he obtains from his local bishop. The marriage was null not because there is anything lacking in a Protestant marriage but because he as a Catholic was bound to observe the Catholic form of marriage. In our law he was considered bound to this law even though he publicly left the Church.

Q. *Recently I noticed a case of where a person who had been married in the Catholic Church and afterwards divorced applied for a church annulment. Before the annulment was issued, the party had met someone and decided to get married again. Although the Church could not marry this couple because of the still legitimacy of the first marriage, the Church had given this couple her "blessing." Could you please explain this blessing?*

A. Some priest may have blessed the couple, but this was not the Church giving an official blessing. If the priest actually witnessed their marriage before two other witnesses and he was a pastor or associate pastor of the place where the exchange of vows took place, then we have an interesting situation.

The priest certainly did wrong, but if the person's first marriage in reality was invalid, then the present union would be valid, even though the Church court had not yet declared the first marriage invalid. The Church does not annul the first marriage; it simply declares it null and void from the beginning if there was something missing in the exchange of vows.

Q. *I have been told I cannot marry the man I love in the Church. He was married before. He loved his wife very much. After only a few months of marriage he was drafted and they were separated. She became lonely, and needing companionship she started running around and dating other men. Soon she wanted her freedom again and served divorce papers on him when he was in Vietnam. When he returned he still wanted to save the marriage but she went ahead with the divorce. Must he suffer because of her? Is there no way we can marry in the Church? What do you suggest we do?*

A. I suggest you urge the man you want to marry to present his case to the marriage court in the diocese in which he lives. His marriage may very well have been invalid.

I find it increasingly difficult to presume that a woman so soon unfaithful as his wife demonstrated herself to be could have committed herself seriously to marriage. Her subsequent actions indicate that she did not consider herself bound to one man. It is very difficult to prove this in our matrimonial courts, especially since in our church law a marriage must be presumed valid until proven invalid.

More and more today, however, our matrimonial judges and church law specialists are growing impatient with a presumption of law which can unjustly bar marriage for persons who in reality are free to marry. The judges cannot change the law, but they can be less demanding in the evidence they require. As a judge myself

I can honestly say that our church courts today are
acutely aware that our marriage court procedures need
to be changed and meanwhile are doing everything
within the law to eliminate as many injustices as possible.
Tell your man that he will find the court sympathetic.
The more cases of this kind that are brought to the attention of our courts and even sent to Rome the sooner
we can expect changes to be made in church laws regulating matrimonial cases.

Q. *My sis is going with a divorced man. He comes from
a family where one of the parents was a Catholic and
has left the Church. His parents left it up to him to
choose the religion he wished and so he went to the
Catholic Church, but was never baptized. He married in
the Catholic Church a woman from whom he is now
divorced. Is there any possibility that my sis could
marry this fellow in the Church?*

A. Yes, it is possible. A recent decree from Rome in-
forms us that under certain conditions a marriage of this
kind can be dissolved. If one party is not baptized then
the marriage is not considered sacramental, even though
a dispensation was granted by the Church. Your sister
should introduce the man to some priest who will assist
him in presenting a petition to the proper church court.
It will take considerable time to prepare this case. There
will have to be certain proof that the man was never
baptized. And the case must be sent to Rome.

Q. *Can a wife get an annulment if she finds she has
unknowingly married a man who is a transvestite?*

A. Why not present your case to a church court and see? The desire to wear the clothes of the opposite sex is a symptom of psychological problems that just may make it impossible for one so bothered to commit oneself to marriage. This is something a Catholic marriage court would have to decide with the help of psychiatrists.

Q. *Do I have sufficient reasons for a marriage annulment? My husband lied to me before our marriage about his previous life. He had been married to a Catholic girl out of the Church. When he met me he took instructions and became a Catholic before our marriage. He lied to the priest who performed our marriage ceremony by saying he had never been married before. I found the marriage certificate after we were married. Before we were married he was in favor of a family, but after the wedding he insisted on any means to avoid children. In spite of this we have a daughter. During pregnancy my husband tried to cause the baby to be aborted. He quit going to church and the sacraments five years after we were married. He has had numerous affairs with other women during 14 years of marriage.*

A. More than likely your marriage is invalid, not because of his previous marriage out of the Church to a Catholic, but because he seemingly denied you the right to have children. His previous marriage would not constitute an impediment to your marriage since it was itself invalid because of the lack of the proper form required by the Church. However, the fact that he lied about this would certainly throw doubt on the sincerity of his willingness to have children before you married him. His subsequent actions would indicate that he did not intend to have children. The fact that a child was conceived in spite of his precautions would not change the situation. You should see a priest who will help you prepare a petition of nullity to be made to your bishop through the proper channels.

"INTERNAL FORUM" SOLUTION

Q. *I married a man who professed a belief in "free love," and for eight years he played the field though married. I couldn't feel that this was a valid marriage and so I divorced him. Two years after that I met a good Christian man, though not a Catholic, and two years later we were married by a justice of the peace. This man, as I do, believes that when two people are married they do indeed become one, forsaking all others. We have been married 16 years, and I do feel that this contract is the valid one.*

*I have talked with my pastor about a Church annulment of the first marriage, but who can prove a party had intentions of doing or not doing any particular thing at the time the contract was entered into? What can I do? I can't give up the successful marriage I am now in and yet I want so much to receive the sacraments.**

A. Present your case to your local Catholic marriage tribunal. It may be that the man's subsequent conduct

*This question and answer previously appeared in *What a Modern Catholic Believes about Moral Problems,* The Thomas More Press, 1971, pp. 54ff.

can be used as evidence that he entered marriage without any intention of being faithful. This is, indeed, hard to prove. You may be encouraged, therefore, to learn that your situation and that of thousands who suffer with you, has in recent years been given serious consideration by moral theologians and that some of these have decided there is a solution for you.

Our Church has long recognized that at times her laws can work hardships on certain individuals and so she admitted the possibility of settling a problem privately that could not be handled publicly by a Church court. What was done in an ecclesiastical court or by a public decision of a bishop was considered done "in the external forum"; what was done privately without any public effect was considered done "in the internal forum."

Hence, for example, a confessor or pastor might be allowed by the Sacred Penitentiary in Rome to absolve a person from an excommunication or impediment in the internal forum and give him the sacraments though publicly or in the external forum the action would have no legal effect—in other words, so far as the public was concerned the excommunication was not lifted.

With this as background, I quote from one of the leading and most influential moral theologians of our time, Father Bernard Haering, C.SS.R., who has this to say:

"There are (marriage) cases in which there is no practical doubt that the first marriage was not made in heaven but because of special circumstances an external forum solution could not be obtained. The penitent is a sincere person; he knows for sure the facts that prove the invalidity of the first marriage; but in view of the complicated canonical procedure he is not able to give the kind of proofs that are required by many ecclesiastical tribunals. If the confessor or pastor or tribunal official feels sure this is the situation, there should be no delay for an internal forum solution. If the persons involved live in a second stable marriage, they should be assured that, in conscience, they can consider their marriage as valid before God. In order to avoid trouble, they should not mention this situation in further confessions."

If you read this carefully, you will see that this possibility does not apply to everyone who "feels" his first marriage was invalid, but only to him who "knows for sure the facts that prove the invalidity of the first marriage." Here are some possibilities: 1) The first marriage seems to be certainly invalid for reasons recognized by Church courts but there is not sufficient proof available; 2) the first marriage seems to be certainly invalid for reasons recognized by Church courts but a final verdict from a Church court cannot be expected for several years; 3) the first marriage is regarded as certainly invalid for a reason which many theologians and Church lawyers acknowledge as sufficient but Church courts do not yet accept.

This problem has been thoroughly discussed in the 1970 issues of *The Clergy Review,* a highly respected monthly published by and for the Roman Catholic clergy of England. In this discussion three English theologians, Fathers James McManus, C.SS.R., Kevin T. Kelly and Henry Allard, S.C.J., and Father J. Boelaars, C.SS.R., of the Academia Alfonsiana in Rome, have agreed in substance with an article of Father Haering written for the *Jurist,* publication of the U.S. Canon Law Society. Father Haering has also published his opinion in Volume 55 of the theological periodical *Concilium.*

All these theologians are careful to point out that they do not think that what they recommend will destroy the Church's position regarding the indissolubility of marriage. Father Haering says: "I have not recommended that a priest be permitted to allow divorced people to remarry or that he should be able to declare a second marriage legally valid.

"My concern is for the credible proclamation of the divine mercy for contrite sinners who in a legally and ecclesiastically regrettable situation are prepared to do the best they can and who sincerely seek God's will."

And Father Kelly: "It is simply trying to maintain a balance between the respect owed to the external forum for the sake of the common good and the right and need of this individual Christian to share in the signs of Christ's forgiveness and redeeming love."

What these theologians now publicly support has for several years been put into practice in some European countries, and here in this country there are retreat masters and parish mission preachers who have been making use of it.

Whether the priests where you live are willing and able to consider this solution for you depends upon local situations and your own attitude. In some places people might be shocked and scandalized by such a solution. Much depends, also, upon the kind of marriage you are now in and how well you have tried to remain faithful to the Church as far as you were able.

Q. *I understand that Rome has issued a decree declaring that bishops may not grant permission for the use of the so-called good conscience solution that permits some remarried couples to receive the sacra-*

*ments even though their marriage cannot be rectified in
the Church. Does this mean that what you once wrote
about the practice of certain confessors who permitted such couples to receive is no longer permissible?*

A. You are referring to the "internal forum" solution
to the problem that confessors use to help some people
who have reasons for thinking their first marriage was
invalid but cannot prove it. I do not think this Roman
decree changes the picture at all. Several U.S. bishops
who wanted to regulate what some confessors in their
dioceses were doing petitioned Rome for permission to
give guidelines to follow and permission to authorize
confessors in certain instances to use the "internal forum"
solution. Well, just as soon as the bishop enters into
the situation it becomes an "external forum" case. The
answer Rome gave was very carefully worded. It made
no reference to the "internal forum" solution. It said
only that bishops must continue to follow the traditional
practice. That referred to the permission bishops have
been giving to such couples to receive the sacraments
provided they live as brother and sister. As I see it,
the very fact that the document made no reference to the
"internal forum" solution indicated that Rome did not
want to condone or condemn the practice and, therefore,
left the door open for experiment.

PAULINE PRIVILEGE

Q. *You recently stated that "if one of the parties to the
marriage was not baptized, then the marriage was not
sacramental and, therefore, can be dissolved." I do
hope you are wrong. I am a Catholic married to a non-*

Catholic who was divorced from a non-baptized person, and for 28 years I have been trying to be married in the Church and have been told it can't be done. I have raised two Catholic children, educated in Catholic schools and college. My spouse has been under instructions to become Catholic and has been refused. If there are new rulings, I would appreciate hearing of them.

A. I can't tell whether you are man or woman, so I shall have to use the awkward word "spouse." If it can clearly be shown that the first spouse of your spouse was never baptized even though your spouse was baptized, then your spouse can be given permission by the Church to enter the Church and by marrying you in the Church dissolve the previous bond of marriage. This is an extension of the Pauline Privilege which the Church has allowed for many years but more generously recently.

The Pauline Privilege, as you know, takes its name from St. Paul, who in I Cor 7:12-15 teaches that a marriage between two unbaptized persons may be dissolved if the husband or wife is converted to the faith while the unbaptized party refuses to live with the convert peacefully. The Church concluded from this that a natural marriage, i.e., one between unbaptized persons, could be dissolved in favor of the faith—meaning that it could be dissolved so that one party would be free to practice his faith.

When it became clear to the Church that a marriage between one baptized and one not baptized was also to be considered a natural marriage and therefore not sacramental, the Church began to grant permission to extend the Pauline Privilege to these cases. But permission to use the privilege in these cases was reserved to

Rome and could not be granted by local bishops.

Twenty-eight years ago Rome was granting these permissions reluctantly. Authorities in the Curia demanded that many witnesses be heard to testify that the one party was certainly not baptized. The process of proof became a great burden upon understaffed chancery offices, especially in small dioceses. Parish priests were instructed not to seek for such permission except in cases where they were sure it would be possible to prove beyond a doubt that the one party was not baptized.

Perhaps in your case the priests you approached decided that because of the lack of cooperative witnesses it would be impossible to satisfy Rome. Perhaps you were in a diocese where the bishop felt his chancery office was unable to process such a case — and there were some. Whatever the case may be, now may be the time to try again. Rome has lessened the demands and is attempting to speed up the process and now would grant the permission to help you practice your faith even though your spouse does not want to become a Catholic.

Q. *My brother-in-law wanted to become a Catholic. After taking all the instructions to become a Catholic, the priest said he had to get a release from his former wife to become a Catholic. They are divorced. He had to get a lawyer to handle this. She refused to give him a release and he could not become a Catholic and therefore he and my sister cannot have their marriage rectified by the Catholic Church. My brother-in-law would make a good Catholic. How come?*

A. What you are referring to, I think, is a possible use of the Pauline Privilege which went awry. This is a privilege granted by the Church to dissolve a marriage bond contracted between two unbaptized persons, after the baptism of one of the spouses and the refusal of the other spouse to cohabit peacefully.

This privilege is based upon the supposition that St. Paul granted this privilege in I Cor 7:12-15 to new Christians whose unbelieving spouses would not live with them. In verse 15 he says: "But if the unbelieving partner desires to separate, let it be so; in such a case the brother or sister is not bound." The Church has interpreted this to mean that the marriage bond between two unbaptized persons is dissolved when the unbaptized spouse refuses to cohabit peacefully and the baptized spouse contracts a sacramental marriage with a baptized person.

You will note that the unbaptized party must refuse to live with the convert. In your case, doubtless, both your brother-in-law and his first wife were unbaptized at the time of their marriage and he would have been given permission to make use of the Pauline Privilege had the first wife refused to live with him. Seemingly she wanted him back. But, did she?

It is unusual in such cases to use a lawyer and a mistake to speak of the "release." The lawyer may not have understood what question he was supposed to give to the woman. If he asked her for a release, this might have been misunderstood. She might have been afraid that she was releasing her former husband from any financial obligations to her. Or she may have refused out of spite so that he could not be properly married in the Catholic Church. In actual fact she may not have wanted to live in peace with your brother-in-law at all.

My suggestion to your brother-in-law would be to

write to the chancery office in the diocese where he lives and ask for a chance to explain his situation.

Q. *Is it possible for a Catholic to marry a divorced unbaptized person who has never gone or belonged to any Protestant Church? His ex-wife was a baptized Methodist, and they were married in the Methodist Church.*

A. The Catholic Church holds such a marriage to be valid, but since one of the parties was not baptized it is not considered sacramental and therefore not held to be indissoluble. The Pope does dissolve such a marriage in favor of the faith.

If the man desires to be baptized in the Catholic Church and marry a Catholic woman, he can petition the Pope to declare the first, non-sacramental, marriage dissolved so that he may practice his new faith. Or if he does not want to join the Church, he may make the petition so that you may continue to practice your faith. You should discuss this case with a priest who will help you present it to the proper authorities. Such a case takes considerable time to prepare, for Rome demands clear proof that the one party was never baptized.

THE DIVORCED LIFE

Q. *Please answer these questions:*

1. Am being sued for divorce (3 years married; no children), think have grounds for an annulment. Where do I go, and whom do I see?

2. If a civil divorce is granted, is it too late to apply for an annulment?

3. Can a young Catholic divorced person attend parties and church dances announced for young people and widowed?

What about the young divorced? There are many people who did not want the divorce. Where do they go? They are not all tramps or bums who like to hang on bars and drink.

A. Go seek advice from your pastor, and get a lawyer. Your pastor can tell you whether there is a possibility that the marriage was invalid or send you to the Church authorities who can help you.

No, it is not too late to seek an annulment after a civil divorce is granted.

Your last question is a heartbreaker. The only answer I can give you is to stay away from parties and dances announced for the single and widowed until you are assured by Church authorities that your marriage was invalid and that you are free to marry. To go to such social events now is to risk dragging another Catholic into the same unfortunate position you now find yourself.

The bar is surely not the answer. God's grace is, if you have the courage to ask for it.

Q. *Some weeks ago, you gave a young divorcee the advice to stay away from single couples' groups and that there was nothing she could do but see her pastor and pray. Good advice, but thanks for nothing.*

This has been the Church's attitude for so many years. Sweep them under the rug. I am in the same boat, only with the added problem of 15 years and six children (the latter really a blessing in disguise). However, times are changing. There is an organization in

*our diocese called the "Judeans" for just such people
as we. They are sponsoring retreats. I attended one of
these, and it was a revelation and a great help. They
offer concrete advice from experience.*

*Please, don't you just brush us off with a "pray,"
when we ask for help. We need prayer, and don't think
it doesn't help, but we are in a very peculiar position as
far as today's society is concerned. I wish I had a nickel
for every time I hear, "O well, you'll marry again," and
often from supposedly good Catholics.*

A.   I wasn't trying to brush off people with your problem.
I honestly felt and still do that a young divorcee should
stay away from church socials for single people, for most
who attend such affairs have marriage in view.

Your own organization seems to offer the best help
possible for those in your predicament, and it is an
example of what the Church can do. Divorced laymen
are part of the Church. What they do to help themselves
will indeed be the Church responding to a peculiar problem of our society.

Q.   *A dear friend of mine has a problem. She married
during high school a boy who was never baptized. Later
they were married in the rectory. Now they have separated and divorced. She has a small child. About six
months ago she wanted to get back into the Church.
She went to a priest for help. He told her she was married and since she obtained a divorce she is excommunicated. There are no signs of her husband's reconciliation. Now she doesn't go to church and her child
probably will not be able to now. Can she not find a way
to get back into the Church? She has not remarried.*

A. Your friend is not excommunicated for obtaining a civil divorce. If it is not her fault that she and her husband cannot be reconciled or if it is impossible for the two to live together in peace and harmony, then she may return to the sacraments. Are you sure you have all the details correct? Maybe your friend didn't explain her case properly to the priest. Tell her to try another priest. It is now possible for a Catholic who married a non-baptized person with a dispensation to obtain, under certain conditions, a dissolution of the marriage from Rome.

Q. *If one party of a Catholic marriage seeks and obtains a divorce for no serious reason after 31 years of marriage, can this person still receive the sacraments of Penance and Communion worthily? I have been told they cannot. Is this true?*

A. After sticking it out for 31 years, the "party" must have had some pretty good reasons for obtaining a divorce. But granted for the sake of argument that there were no serious reasons, the party could now be sorry for the action, repent and return to a worthy reception of the sacraments.

If it is possible, however, to restore the marriage, then the party could only show true sorrow by demonstrating a willingness to resume married life. If the other party is willing, this will require the obtaining of a new marriage license and the renewal of vows to satisfy civil requirements. Perhaps this is the case, and the party refused and for this reason you were told that he (she) could not receive the sacraments worthily.

Q. *Is a Catholic man divorced from a Catholic woman*

and remarried civilly bound in conscience to remember
his divorced unremarried wife in his will if she has an
independent income of her own? Also would the di-
vorced wife be bound to remember her remarried
spouse in her will?

A. A divorce frees a couple from any legal obligation to
each other. There might be a moral obligation—in other
words, an obligation before God—to leave something to
help support a destitute divorced spouse, but in the case
you describe I can see no reason why there is any strict
obligation. The noble and more Christian thing to do
would be to remember the first wife in some way.

Q. *My wife asked me this question several times: What*
happens when a wife remarries, who is the man she
spends eternity with? Can you answer this?

A. The only answer I can give is the one the Sadducees
got when they tried to argue with Jesus about belief in the
resurrection. The Sadducees, who denied the possibility of
the resurrection, tried to make Jesus look ridiculous by
posing the problem of a woman married successively to
seven brothers.

"Now, at the resurrection to which of these will she
be wife since she had been married to all seven?" they
asked.

Jesus replied: "The children of this world take wives
and husbands, but those who are judged worthy of a
place in the other world and in the resurrection from the
dead do not marry because they can no longer die, for
they are the same as angels, and being children of the
resurrection they are sons of God" (Lk 20:27-37).

So keep your chin up. You and any possible successor are not apt to be rivals in heaven. But just what is on your wife's mind?

Q. *Would it be possible for you to explain that Catholics are not excommunicated if they obtain a civil divorce? In my work with the Judean Society (an association of divorced Catholic women) I continually find divorced women who have been away from the sacraments for years because they thought they were excommunicated due to divorce. Another thing that might help bring people back to the Church is an explanation of general confession.*

A.   There is no excommunication attached to obtaining a civil divorce. If one had serious reasons for doing so, it would not be sinful to obtain a divorce; it might even be an obligation. However, many dioceses have a law obliging a Catholic to obtain permission from the bishop before seeking a divorce. To disobey such a law knowingly would be sinful.

I am not so sure that I go along with you on the general confession. This is a confession in which one reviews his life or the time since his last retreat during the time of a spiritual retreat or at a time when he begins a new phase of his life, such as before marriage. This is a confession of devotion which the penitent prepares himself for with considerable meditation and introspection.

Those who have been away from the sacraments for some time have a different problem. The more they prepare for the confession the harder it becomes. To them I advise: let the confessor do the work. After a preparation of prayer and an act of sorrow, go into the confessional, tell the priest how long it has been approximately since the last confession, and then say, "Help me." It's that easy.

The Judean Society merits the attention of all those Catholic divorced women who need spiritual and human consolation to live with their problem. I am happy to give the mailing address: The Judean Society, Inc., 756 Lois Avenue, Sunnyvale, California 94087.

part 7

Sex and Sin

Sex and Sin

THE SEXUAL SCENE

Q. *Several months ago I subscribed to a well-known book of the month club. Although they distribute some fine books, others are very outspoken on sex. Is it a sin to read these books? I have not received Communion for the last few Sundays because I am uncertain about this.*

A. If the books are an occasion of sin for you, certainly you should not read them. Most such clubs offer a choice of selection or rejection. You do not have to take everything that is offered, so exercise some judgment.

But perhaps you are being overly scrupulous. The bible, too, is "outspoken" about sex. If you have in mind the current spate of popular novels that are crammed with sex episodes described explicitly and ad nauseam, then I would say you are guilty at least of wasting your time.

Since you are troubled, talk the matter over in confession and get back to Communion.

Q. *I read* Playboy *magazine every month. In the let-*

ters to the editor column I have repeatedly seen letters of praise from clergymen, most recently that of one "Reverend Father." Is the magazine something Catholics should consider laudable?

A. Hardly. Defenders of the magazine are fond of pointing out that it often publishes worthwhile articles or comment on political and social issues. These are incidental or accidental. They have nothing to do with the real purpose or push behind the publication.

I must confess that I speak from secondhand knowledge. I am not a reader of the magazine but its presence, contents and influence have not escaped the attention of clergymen and moralists. A very fine, comprehensive analysis of "Playboyism," written by John McLaughlin, S.J., can be found in the May, 1968, issue of *St. Anthony Messenger*. To it I am indebted for the following analysis.

Several reputable psychologists have attributed *Playboy's* appeal to a search for male identity in an age in which the traditional husband-father image has been emasculated. To the rootless, valueless, aimless male the magazine offers glossy guidelines. It tells the reader what to wear, what car to drive, where the smart places are. Most importantly, it teaches him how to cultivate the manner of sophisticated detachment which is crucial to the playboy identity.

This detachment pervades the magazine's view of sexuality. A true playboy never commits himself to a permanent alliance or even to any involvement beyond the physical. Woman is considered a plaything, a purely transitory object to be discarded when the season or the mood changes.

For those to whom the "good life" is as yet unattainable, *Playboy* provides fantasy in the form of nudity. Thus the appeal to the teenage male. In reality, the whole *Playboy* "image" is based on protracted immaturity. There is an ill-concealed effeminacy that comes out in the consuming interest in clothes, accessories, scents and surroundings; true virility is denigrated in the overriding concern with a sex dreamland.

Commercially successful, *Playboy* is. Laudable? No.

Q. *During a recent conversation the subject of pornography was discussed especially since a recent newspaper article quoted a Protestant minister as saying it was "therapeutic." I mentioned that I had heard at one time that one of the largest collections of pornography was housed in the Vatican. Please tell me if you can if this is true and if so what possible reason can be given for this. Also what is your reaction to the so-called therapeutic value of pornography?*

A.   It all depends upon what you mean by pornography. Years ago I was told by fellow seminarians in Boston that their bishop, Cardinal O'Connell, had trouble retrieving photos sent him from Rome of Michelangelo's Sistine Chapel frescoes of Adam and Eve which had been confiscated by customs officials as indecent. If the nude or partially nude human body, sculpture or painting, is considered pornographic, then the Vatican has an ample supply of pornography in its museums, the Sistine Chapel and even St. Peter's Basilica in which there are statues of bare-bosomed female figures portraying the virtues. Perhaps some puritanical traveler concluded that all this was pornography and this is the basis of your information. I know of no other.

I know nothing about the therapeutic value of pornography. That is out of my line. But I suspect that talk of its therapeutic value is pure hokum.

Q. *Some time ago a man asked you a question concerning mini-skirts and dresses. The reply does not in any way resemble one that would be given by a member of the cloth. The man was told if he wanted to speak out against the mini style he had more nerve than you. If you don't have the nerve to speak out against sin and evil, then you should lay aside your priestly robes.*

Granting that the mini is a style, as you pointed out, Christian women should not wear them or anything that could cause a man to stumble.

A. Dear Madam: I shall try to answer you with gentlemanly constraint. Could it be that you misjudge men by implying that they must necessarily stumble at the sight of a pretty leg?

I don't consider the mini-skirt an evil. It might have been evil for some when first it appeared, but like every other daring change in women's fashions (the skirt that shockingly exposed ankles for the first time!) men got used to it. I have lived long enough to learn that it is a waste of energy to speak out against the evils of women's dress, for by the time people begin to listen, the dress is no longer evil.

MASTURBATION

Q. *Is masturbation a serious sin or is it a sin at all? This question was raised at a church meeting, but not answered to anyone's satisfaction.*

A. I'm not surprised. It isn't the kind of question that can be discussed satisfactorily at a church meeting. But it is a question that bothers many people. Yours is the 32nd request I have received in recent weeks to discuss it.

The old manuals of moral theology taught that willful masturbation (or "complete sexual satisfaction obtained by some source of self-stimulation," as it was described) was always a serious sin. The manuals did recognize that individual acts were not always seriously sinful when full consent of the will was lacking.

Theologians today are taking a new look at the problem in the light of new knowledge of psychology and sex. Some experts feel that while the teaching of the manuals is correct, it does not give enough attention to the many influences which reduce or remove one's freedom in performing this act, and, therefore, reduce the sinfulness involved. They point out that while a person may knowingly and, in a sense, willingly masturbate, this action may be brought on by any number of physical and/or psychological pressures which reduce the freedom of choice which is necessary for serious sin. They cite studies in which it is shown that many instances of masturbation occur when the person is tense, depressed, or extremely tired. These pressures, they say, can and frequently do limit the freedom of the act, and so not every act of masturbation, even when performed consciously, would be seriously sinful.

Others point out that the practice of masturbation is the rule, rather than the exception, among adolescents and that often the youth confessing masturbation has not broken off his relationship of love with God and neighbor, which is, after all, what serious sin is all about.

Q. *I have a problem that is making something close to a nervous wreck out of me. I don't feel as if I could go to a priest in a confessional and tell him; so I am imploring you to please help me.*

I don't feel terribly secure at home, but that is only part of the problem. Some time ago I began masturbating. I kept it up but stopped recently. I don't know if it is a mortal sin so I haven't been to Communion in a while. Each Sunday when I go to church I pray to God to give me strength, and I feel he has. I want very, very badly to go to Communion again, but don't feel as if I have the right.

Please help me and tell me if I have been sinning. I want so much to be able to receive Communion again. I am a girl.

A. Don't make your problem more difficult than it is. Go to confession and simply say: "I fell into the practice of masturbating for (so many) months. With God's help I have stopped." The priest won't think you are somebody awful. Your problem is not unique.

Only God knows whether what you did was seriously sinful or not. In young people going through adolescence more than likely such actions are not serious sins each time they happen. Serious sin might spring from an attitude toward the problem of "I don't care" and a refusal to struggle against the tendency. It doesn't pay to be too easy on yourself in this matter, though. In practice the safest thing to do is to be sorry for the actions as though they were serious.

The procuring of sexual pleasure by oneself and for oneself alone is basically something extremely selfish. It is to use for self alone something that is to be shared with another in marriage, something which makes it possible to give self to another. To give in to this inclination and develop a habit of masturbation might very well harm your future life in marriage, for your attitude toward sex would be selfish instead of self-giving, as it should be for happiness in marriage.

The best antidote for your problem would seem to be to get out of yourself, stop feeling sorry for yourself, get busy about the needs of others; every day try to do something special for a friend or for those living or working with you.

The only way to do this is to be humble, admit you need God's grace to overcome your selfishness. You need the help of the graces that come from frequent reception of Holy Communion. So, get to confession right away and start over.

The insecurity you feel about your home life may be more serious than you realize and more than likely had something to do with your problem. You should seek help. Talk to a priest or a sister or a doctor you know or to anyone else with whom you can open up.

Q. *Am I correct in thinking that a married couple may practice birth control by the rhythm method without committing sin? If so, why cannot a single fellow get relief from masturbation if he observes the same number of days of denial as the married couple making use of the rhythm method?*

A. What the married couple performs is an act of love, a mutual giving of self. Masturbation is an act of selfishness, a turning in on self. If you can't distinguish the difference, you are too dense to be capable of sin.

Q. *I am an "old maid," aged 45, who had been jilted earlier in life and, as fate willed, just never found the right man. I still have strong desires, however, and since I have no other outlet, I revert to masturbation. Is this a grave sin? I've read articles that say "no," but yet my conscience bothers me terribly for days afterward. If it's still considered a mortal sin, please give suggestions on how to avert the act. I've tried everything, including my own strong penance.*

Q. *My husband died a few months ago. We were married many years and I am just past the childbearing age. Is masturbation wrong for me? Although one part of me feels it is not wrong, as it hurts no one, another part wants to know for sure. It is only occasional and does relieve some of the tensions and loneliness.*

A. I have received a number of similar letters from lonely widows and widowers who have the same problem and other letters inquiring whether or not the Church has changed its teaching on the sinfulness of masturbation.

The manuals of moral theology have traditionally taught that one who willfully and with full knowledge of the sinfulness of what he is doing commits a serious sin when he obtains complete sexual satisfaction by some source of self-stimulation. But these authors knew enough about human nature to recognize that acts of masturbation very often were not fully deliberate. They taught that persons in a sleepy state just after awakening or trying to get to sleep were not in complete control of their actions. They were aware that a habit contracted in youth might become so overpowering that a person trying to overcome it would not be fully free and therefore not guilty of sin each time he failed.

It is true that theologians today are taking a new look at the problem of masturbation in the light of new knowledge of psychology and sex. As I wrote in another answer: "Some experts feel that while the teaching of the manuals is correct, it does not give enough attention to the many influences which reduce or remove one's freedom in performing this act, and therefore, reduce the sinfulness involved. They point out that while a person may knowingly and, in a sense, willingly masturbate, this action may be brought on by any number of physical and/or psychological pressures which reduce the freedom of choice which is necessary for serious sin. They cite studies in which it is shown that many instances of masturbation occur when the person is tense, depressed, or extremely tired. These pressures, they say, can and frequently do limit the freedom of the act, and so not every act of masturbation, even when performed consciously, would be seriously sinful.

"Others point out that the practice of masturbation is the rule, rather than the exception, among adolescents and that often the youth confessing masturbation has not broken off his relationship of love with God and neighbor, which is, after all, what serious sin is all about." This may apply to a number of lonely older people.

I concluded the answer: "As a practical suggestion, I recommend that a person confronted with the problem of masturbation look into his heart as honestly as he can and try to discover the reasons for his acts. If he finds that masturbation is one symptom of a generally self-centered life and that, in many other ways as well, he consistently tends to prefer his own well-being and pleasure to the demands of God and neighbor, then he may well be concerned about his moral situation. If, on the other hand, he discovers that his occasional acts of masturbation, which he may consider morally wrong in themselves, are out of character with the rest of his life and that they do not change his general relationship of love and concern for God and neighbor, then he may conclude that the individual acts are not seriously sinful and may look upon them as reminders that he is a sinful human in constant need of God's help to overcome sinful tendencies. This same rule of thumb may be applied by those who from a long habit fail more frequently."

Prayer and self-discipline are two essentials for overcoming the habit. But sometimes a physician should be consulted for bladder problems or other physical irritations that might be the cause of the difficulty—especially in the case of older people. Also it is essential to keep busy working and living for others.

PROBLEMS OF PURITY

Q. *I'm a man, 66 years old. Purity, or lack of it, has always been my number-one problem. By daily Mass and Communion and confession every two weeks I managed to cope with it—until about one and a half years ago. Suddenly I began to have an almost steady flow of impure thoughts and fantasies. Some I resisted, more I gave in to. I had a long talk with a priest, followed by confession. He said he didn't think I was guilty of mortal sin. The thoughts persisted and also my indulgence in most of them. However, I did continue to go to Holy Communion daily. I mentioned this in confession to another priest who told me not to be troubled, but to continue to receive daily. At later confessions to other priests I still mentioned the problem. Some said nothing. Two others said I should not have received while in a state of serious sin. To one I said I wasn't sure—meaning that I wasn't positive of serious guilt in light of previous advice. What should I do?*

A. For just once try to look at yourself as though you were looking at a stranger described in your picture of yourself. Here is a man who wants to serve God, who goes to Mass and Communion daily. He doesn't want to offend God. He is alarmed at the thought that he might have offended him by giving in to evil thoughts. This can only mean that he still wants to love God. If he weren't worried about the thoughts, if he did not care one way or another, there might be some doubt about whether he cared about God. But this is not so in the case at hand.

Put it another way. A man has been faithful to his wife for over 40 years. He suddenly finds another woman living in the same neighborhood attractive. He finds it very difficult to stop thinking of her. He goes out of his way to avoid her, but still he keeps thinking of her. Meanwhile, he does everything he can to show his wife he still loves her. The thoughts of the other woman actually make him more aware of his obligations to his wife. Is he unfaithful to his wife? Of course not.

Mortal sin is being unfaithful to God, telling him you want no part of him. It is not so much any one act as the state of being an enemy of God. You are not in a state of mortal sin. You are doing the best you can to fight those thoughts that bother you. If you have any doubts about whether you sin by giving in to them, be sure that they are not serious sins. The first priests who gave you advice were correct. The two others probably did not understand your situation clearly. Go to confession regularly for the purpose of obtaining the grace to keep on fighting the temptations. Tell the confessor that you are struggling against those temptations, and you mention them only in case there was any sin involved. But don't go into details.

The less attention you pay to this problem of yours, the sooner it will disappear. Laugh it off. Tell yourself you are human like the rest of men and learn to laugh at yourself. And when you prepare for Communion, don't worry about the thoughts and feelings that are beyond your control, but rather about whether you have loved your fellowmen as you should.

Q. *I am a single person in my late 60's and have frequent thoughts about chastity and never seem to be able to make up my mind if they are willful or not. Do I have to go to confession before receiving Holy Communion?*

A. If you can't make up your mind about whether you sin from these thoughts, then you are in doubt, and whenever you are in doubt you have not sinned seriously and therefore not in need of confession. Go to Communion, recognizing that you are weak and in need of closer union with Christ.

ADULTERY

Q. *I'm writing to you in desperation. I've been unfaithful to my husband; I'd feel real well if I could tell him the truth. But I can't. I can't show love for him, but still we have to stay together. I'm not being fair to him. In a sense I may love him; I don't know. But I know if I told him I was unfaithful I'd feel better. I have nothing to lose. Do you think I should tell him? I believe he suspects something is wrong.*

A. Tell the confessor in the sacrament of Penance what you have done and resolve that you will never do it again. But keep your mouth shut at home. Work hard at reviving your love for your husband, let him know you need him; that's the only way you will ever dispel the suspicions.

Q. *If a Catholic divorced person has an affair with a Catholic single person, are both parties guilty of adultery or just the divorced person? If the divorced person is the only one guilty of adultery, what is the single person guilty of?*

A. They are both guilty of adultery—so long as one of them has a living spouse.

Q. *I would like your opinion on a subject which has been a source of controversy in our family.*

I am under the impression that the sin of adultery has been committed by a married person when any kind of physical intimacy is involved with a person other than the marriage partner—that intercourse need not take place. I realize that in the eyes of the law this would not be considered as such, but in the Church it is adultery and must be confessed as such. Am I right in this belief?

A. No. The sin of adultery carries the legal implications of the term: complete intimate unfaithfulness to one's marriage partner. Lesser degrees of physical intimacy certainly can be sinful, both in themselves and because they might lead to adultery.

Q. *Two of the Ten Commandments have me puzzled: the second and the sixth. Why is it you can curse up a blue streak time and time again and still go to confession and Communion, but if you commit adultery time after time again you cannot receive the sacraments? Why is one of these commandments so much greater than the other?*

A. Adultery is an offense against the rights of another. What is more it is an act that usually is committed not on the spur of the moment but with some deliberation and foresight. Cursing a "blue streak" is usually something that is not seriously meant, performed by persons who are carried away with anger or who from force of habit say things they did not plan to say.

Adultery is a serious sin, and those who commit it time after time are obviously living in the proximate occasion of sin, from which they must remove themselves if they are sincere in their repentance and seek the sacraments. Cursing a "blue streak" is not a serious sin.

Q. *A friend of mine wants to know if it's a sin to have a love affair without marriage. He is a widower who is having an affair with a widow, and he argues that because both he and she once received the sacrament of Matrimony they can now have an affair and it is not sinful. He is waiting for your answer.*

A. Well, let's not keep him waiting long. He's sinning, and he knows it. You are gullible, and he's putting you on. They both had marriage licenses for their previous marriages, but these don't entitle them to consider themselves married to each other, do they?

The sacrament of Matrimony bound them to their previous spouses. Those bonds were broken by death. They are free to marry but not free to act as though they are until they have vowed themselves together in a new sacrament of Matrimony.

Q. *I have a fervent desire to continually receive the Eucharist on Sundays, and since I have only been to confession three times in 25 years, I wonder if I am doing right since I have been separated these many years and live with a man whom I have no desire to marry. I told this to a priest and he said I did not have to decide to change after living in this situation for so long, and since I have not expressed a desire to ever kill someone, it would be all right to continue receiving the Eucharist but to keep praying. I am confused as to the right or wrong in this matter.*

A. The Lord Jesus, whom you desire to be one with the Eucharist, was kind and forgiving to sinners. He forgave the woman caught in adultery, but he did tell her to "Go and sin no more." We must approach the Eucharist with love, and for love to be sincere it must include the determination to do what Jesus wants. "If you love me, keep my commandments," applies to you as to everyone else.

You either got some very bad advice or you interpreted what the priest said to fit your own wishes. It will be very difficult to break this attachment, but what is impossible for us unaided is possible with God's grace. You must decide which you love more, the man you say you don't want to marry or the Eucharistic Lord you say you fervently desire.

Q. *In my office there is an attractive, charming girl who is married and went to Catholic schools. Today, she quite openly arranged an adulterous rendezvous over the office telephone. How am I supposed to react?*

A. Pray for her. And for the future stop eavesdropping on the telephone conversations of attractive, charming girls.

Q. *I am not a Catholic; my husband and four children are. For the last couple of years my husband has been having an affair. I've hung on because I love him, and he says he loves me above anyone, but I'm slowly giving up and frankly feel that I'm about ready to be institutionalized. What I'm really writing for is to say that every Sunday he takes the children to church and they all go to Communion. I don't know all about his religion, but I thought this was wrong. He says it isn't because he has no guilt feelings about having an affair. Please help me.*

A. Your husband knows that what he is doing is sinful and that he should not receive Communion. He is joining the children, I suspect, because he doesn't know what to tell them if they ask him why he doesn't receive. I recommend you see the pastor of the church your husband attends. Tell him your problem. He may be able to help you both.

Q. *If a person gets a divorce and then remarries, he cannot receive the sacraments. But if a husband or wife commits adultery regularly and goes to confession the Church permits them to receive Communion. It would seem their case would be the same as the divorced and remarried. I have this problem at my home with my husband. He does this and goes to confession.*

A. Unless your husband is determined to give up relations with the other woman, his confessions are a mockery and he is living in sin and has no right to receive Communion. His condition may be much worse than some of the Catholics who are in a second marriage which keeps them from the sacraments. They regret what they did but because of children they must rear in a proper home of love and security find it impossible to solve their dilemma.

Q. *I have a co-worker who is having an affair. He goes to Communion every Sunday. I talked to him about this and he answered by saying he confesses in the Penitential Rite of the Mass so he is forgiven. I know for a fact he goes to his mistress the next day. I thought you were forgiven only if you promised to at least try not to commit the sin again. He has a wife and family. What can I tell him to get him to change? I consider myself a friend.*

A. You are right. There is no forgiveness even in the sacrament of Penance for one who is not sincerely determined to give up the sin he confesses. Your friend is mistaken about the Penitential Rite of the Mass. It is not meant as an act of forgiveness of sin but as a preparation for the union with Christ in Mass that does forgive those sins for which the sacrament of Penance is not required.

Those aware of living in a state of serious sin are obliged to amend their lives and confess their sin in the sacrament of Penance before they can worthily receive Holy Communion. You can remind your friend of this, but there is little else you can do except pray that he receive the grace to recognize what a hypocrite he is.

HOMOSEXUALITY

Q. *A non-Catholic friend showed me a newspaper story concerning the marriage of two male homosexuals in a Catholic chapel in Rotterdam, Holland. The marriage supposedly was performed by a priest. As you can see by the enclosed clipping a priest is shown saying Mass and the men are kneeling in front of him. The whole business shocked me. Can this be true? Would the Church marry homosexuals?*

A. Of course not. The Church does not and would not sanction a homosexual "marriage." The story implies the priest may have been "tricked" into this peculiar situation. I have no idea. But certainly no priest would have the right to witness any exchange of vows between two men or bless such a union.

The story smacks of sensational reporting befitting the type of publication in which it appears.

Q. *I am a high school student and very confused. Would you consider being a homosexual a sin? A couple of my very best friends are and it worries me. I really don't consider them that, but many people do.*

I see them as my friends, not as homosexuals. Can you help us?

A. Being a homosexual is not a sin, but giving in to homosexual tendencies would be. People who are attracted in a wrong manner to members of their own sex may not be able to change themselves, but they can with the help of God learn to control their desires just as a normal person can learn to control desires for the opposite sex. The problem is greater for the homosexual, however, for people of the same sex are more often thrown together and more intimately than are persons of the opposite sex.

Such people are lonely and frequently frustrated because of their affliction. If you are sure that your friends are not attracted to you in the wrong way, you may be able to help them by giving them the opportunity for a healthy friendship they need so badly. You must have many other friends, however, and as much as possible be with the two who have problems in the company of others. The greatest assistance you can be to them is to help them associate with normal people and be accepted. It is non-acceptance that drives them to look for others with a similar affliction.

Q. *I am 17 years old and want to know why the Catholic Church frowns on homosexuality. I am a homosexual, many times being proud of it and other times feeling bad. The time I felt bad was when I went to confession and was told by a priest that being gay is a sin. But if this is what I want and wish to live this way, why does the Church say it is bad? I am a good Catholic, attend church every week and receive the Eucharist at least once a month. And I'm gay. I am a homosexual as well as a heterosexual. Can't something be done to allow me and so many like me to remain both gay and good Catholics?*

A.   The Church opposes homosexuality to preserve the likes of you from a life of frustration and unhappiness. You may not be a homosexual at all. From what you say about being heterosexual also, I suspect you are not.

D. J. West, in a Penguin Book study, *Homosexuality,* says: "Many young men who practice homosexuality in their late teens or early twenties grow out of the habit after meeting a suitable woman and settling down to heterosexual life. These are not true homosexuals harboring deep-rooted and intractable inhibitions with regard to the opposite sex; they are simply late starters in heterosexuality." The author adds something that may reassure you: "Provided the young person shows no tendency to adopt manners and habits more appropriate to a member of the opposite sex, and provided he has no special aversion to mixed company, then permanent sexual deviation need not be anticipated."

You are not going to be happy in the "gay life." The name is a complete misnomer. Homosexuals are always going to be a small minority forced to recreate among those who share their same tastes, and this means they are doomed to live restricted, abnormal lives. There is a trend today toward more tolerance and sympathy for homosexuals. But as the expert quoted says: "Tolerance toward homosexuals is not the same as encouragement. No doctor should advise a young person to rest content with a homosexual orientation without first giving a grave warning about the frustration and tragedy that so often attend this mode of life."

Q. *What can you tell a 20-year-old who is engaged in homosexual activity and does not feel he is sinning against God or harming himself?*

A. Urge him to see a psychiatrist.

Q. *I will phrase my twofold question in this manner: From homosexual to saint, possible? From homosexual to normal living male, possible?*

A. A true, inborn homosexual has an enormously heavy cross to bear. If, with the grace of God, that will not be denied him, he heroically lives up to the Christian moral code and directs his sexual energy into charity for others, he can become a saint.

Your other question is beyond my competence; it should be directed to medical experts. I am told by psychiatrists that a number of young people pass through a homosexual phase of life without permanent ill effect. These can become normal living males. But they say that inborn homosexuals are rarely helped. If you have problems, get psychiatric help while you are still young.

RAPE

Q. *If a woman is threatened with death at the point of a gun or knife by a sexual attacker would she be guilty of mortal sin if she submitted? I wonder about this because in being told the stories of certain martyrs as a child, I found that teachers would point out that some saints chose death rather than offend God. But if they were forced would this offend God?*

A. No, if they were forced they couldn't offend God. No woman is obliged to risk her life to ward off such an attack.

The saints you referred to were all young girls, who doubtless felt they would be guilty of sin unless they resisted. Maria Goretti, for example, who is honored as a martyr to purity because of her death at the hands of an attacker in 1902, was only 12 years old and had never been to school. She was killed by a neighbor boy who had for some time attempted to seduce her. She resisted him when he came at her finally with a dagger. She was certainly heroic, but she would not have offended God had she saved her life by submitting to the unjust attack.

Q. *I am most upset by one aspect of the new medical code voted on by the U.S. Catholic Bishops. According to our diocesan newspaper, scraping of the womb after rape is considered a procedure amounting to abortion and is forbidden. I have always understood that such a practice was accepted by the Church. It seems to me that the bishops have taken the principle of reverence for life (which I support) to a ridiculous extreme whereby they would punish the innocent because of a fertilized egg that may or may not be there.*

Conception often takes place after intercourse: are we to let the sperm remain and thereby by our lack of action cause pregnancy after rape? Catholic opponents of abortion have often stated that if proper medical procedures were used after rape, there would be virtually no pregnancies resulting from rape. The bishops' stand seems to me to be brutal, harsh and un-Christian.

A. Traditional Catholic moral books teach that a victim

of rape "may use any effective means to eject or destroy the sperm provided this is done before conception takes place." She may use "a spermicidal, vaginal douche as quickly after rape as possible." This is the opinion of Charles J. McFadden, O.S.A., in his *Medical Ethics,* a textbook for Catholic nurses and premedical students.

Father McFadden explains his position: "Once conception has taken place a new and innocent life has come into existence. This newly created person is guilty of no offense and its inalienable right to life cannot be infringed upon in any way." There are reputable Catholic theologians today who would not agree with this conviction that the fertilized ovum is immediately a person. Dr. Andre E. Hellegers of the Georgetown University School of Medicine, presented some interesting facts in an article on fetal development in the March, 1970, issue of *Theological Studies.* He reported that today it is known that up till the 14th day twins or triplets may be recombined into one single individual and that humans whose genetic type is XX-XY are recombinations into one human being of the products of more than one fertilization. What happens to the extra souls that must be there if the creation of the soul takes place at the moment of conception? I have no intention of going any deeper into this. I mention it only to indicate that there are sound reasons why many theologians and respected Catholic physicians question some of the traditional Catholic medical ethics and are not satisfied with the revised directives for Catholic health facilities issued by the Catholic Hospital Association and approved by the U.S. Bishops.

Since there is considerable doubt whether a person exists at the moment of fertilization, and there is still greater doubt that there is a fertilization at all, it would seem that the very clear rights of the victim of rape should be safeguarded by a D and C (dilation and curettage).

The bishops took a hard line primarily because of the frenzied efforts today to promote abortion in many parts of the country. This is understandable. The preamble of the new document, however, does admit that the directives "might be modified as scientific investigation and theological development open up new problems or cast new light on old ones. I predict that the directives will be modified in the very near future.

BIRTHRIGHT

CONTRACEPTION
JOHN J. NOONAN

HUMAN LIFE
JOHN F DEREK
SHEED & WARD 1972

THE JUDEAN SOCIETY, INC.
756 LOIS AVENUE
SUNNYVALE CA 94087